John R. Lange
4400 Memorial Drive #2008
Houston, Texas 77007

Wooden Toys and Games

Chilton Book Company
Radnor, Pennsylvania

Wooden Toys and Games

Ralph F. Parkison

•

Library of Congress Cataloging in Publication Data

Parkison, Ralph F., 1932–
Wooden toys and games.
Includes index.
1. Wooden toy making. I. Title.
TT174.5.W6P38 1983 745.592   83-70775
ISBN 0-8019-7295-7 (pbk.)

Contents

●

Introduction

•

This book was written because making toys is fun. Its aim is to acquaint the hobbyist with the techniques of constructing toys and to offer both hobbyist and experienced woodworker the plans for a number of toys and games. All the projects are fun to build and display, and children enjoy playing with them. There are a number of well-written books on woodworking and toymaking. This book, however, confines the discussion to small and medium-size toys made from Eastern hard maple. The instructions assume that the hobbyist is familiar with the use of the table saw (variety saw), radial arm saw, jointer, sanders, and other power woodworking tools.

A practical reason for making wooden toys is to have something of lasting value. Making toys also has the potential of producing income. But most importantly, it is a hobby that is fun and a source of individual pride. The satisfaction of fabricating a wooden toy in a short period of time and working with your hands (with the assistance of power tools) can give one a strong feeling of accomplishment.

Tools

To build the toys in this book properly, the hobbyist should be prepared to invest in, or have easy access to, a few basic power tools. This investment does not have to be extensive.

Eastern hard maple is difficult to work using only hand tools. Therefore, hand tools alone are not recommended for the construction of the toys in this book. If you decide to offer your products for sale commercially, then a complete workshop should be established. This may involve a substantial investment, but it will eventually prove worthwhile.

The power tools required for these projects have not been identified according to brand name. With the great number of tools available, it is not always easy to tell which is the best buy for the money. Also, personal preference enters into the selection. Your power tools need not be the most expensive available, but they should be adequate to meet the project needs. There are a number of companies that produce power tools that will do a professional job and will last for years without needing replacement.

Hand tool requirements in the shop will vary according to the projects being built and should be purchased to supplement power equipment. You will definitely need a variety of bar clamps and C clamps for assembly. However, it is a waste of money to arbitrarily buy tools without having a definite need for them.

The toys illustrated here were constructed with the power tools and attachments listed below. The sequence in which they are listed is not necessarily the order in which they should be purchased. Instead, this list is intended to give the hobbyist an idea of the tools most often used in a small woodworking shop.

1. Planer mill (optional): Used to mill rough 1″ hardwood to a smooth $\frac{13}{16}$″ thickness. Hardwood can usually be purchased already milled.

2. Radial arm saw (12″): Used to rough cut lumber to desired lengths before jointing one edge of the woodstock. Precision cutting can also be done on this tool.
   Attachments: 12″ combination saw blade.

3. Jointer (6″): Used to make straight, flat edges on pieces of rough woodstock before cutting parts to exact dimensions on the table saw or radial arm saw.

4. Table saw (variety saw) (10″): Used to cut wood parts to exact dimensions after jointing at least one edge of the milled woodstock. The saw will make square cuts, rectangular cuts, beveled cuts, and angular cuts.
   Attachments: Miter; ripping fence; combination saw blade; dado head.

5. Band saw (14″): Used to cut irregular shaped parts such as wheels and fenders.
   Attachments: $\frac{1}{4}$″ and $\frac{3}{8}$″ band saw blades.

6. Disc sander (12″): Used for final shaping of irregular shaped parts such as wheels and fenders.

7. Drill press (16″): Used to drill holes of all sizes and for drum sanding.
   Attachments: Drill bits ($\frac{1}{4}$″, $\frac{3}{8}$″, $\frac{1}{2}$″, 1″, $1\frac{1}{2}$″); hole saws ($1\frac{1}{4}$″, $1\frac{5}{8}$″, $2\frac{1}{4}$″, $2\frac{1}{2}$″); plug cutters ($\frac{1}{4}$″, $\frac{3}{8}$″, $\frac{1}{2}$″); drum sanders (1″, $1\frac{1}{2}$″, 2″).

8. Belt sander (6″): Used to finish all flat surfaces and to form odd shapes.

9. Belt sander (1″): Used to sand small areas and corners that the 6″ belt sander cannot reach.

10. Wood lathe (12″); a set of hand lathe tools: Used to shape cylindrical objects.

11. Router and homemade shaper table: Used to remove sharp edges and corners and to decorate surfaces.
    Attachments: Rounding bits as desired.

12. Saber saw: Used to cut inside curves.
    Attachments: Saber saw blades as needed.

13. Portable electric drill ($\frac{3}{8}$″): Used to drill $\frac{1}{4}$″ dowel holes to reinforce butt joints.
    Attachments: $\frac{1}{4}$″ speed bit.

14. Orbital sander: Used to finish sanding the exterior surface of each toy.

The Shop

The size of the woodworking shop and the flow of the work as it moves through the production process can make a difference in the quality and quantity of items produced. The efficiency of work flow from the raw or rough wood to the finished product depends upon the arrangement of power equipment and its use in the shop. Figure I–1 shows a reasonably efficient shop arrangement for toys and other small wood projects. This shop permits one major direction of movement, from rear to front, or from unfinished wood to the finished product. There is a certain amount of side-to-side movement of material, from one piece of equipment to another. This type of movement is normal for a small shop. Large production shops may have a nearly straight line or assembly line type of movement.

The following construction operations are common to all of the projects presented in this book. Each step is part of the flow of work illustrated in Figure I–1. You will find that the similarity of construction steps among the projects is an aid to manufacturing the toys smoothly and efficiently.

1. Select the woodstock for production work.
2. If necessary, mill the woodstock to $\frac{13}{16}''$ thickness. One-inch rough Eastern maple is often commercially milled to $\frac{13}{16}''$ thick and is fine for constructing the toys in this book.
3. Place the woodstock on a work table and draw or trace in the parts of the project.
4. Cut the parts of the project to rough lengths on the radial arm saw.
5. Joint the edges of the woodstock on the jointer.
6. Cut the parts of the project to rectangular shapes on the table saw.
7. Cut out the irregular shaped parts on the band saw.
8. Drill all needed holes on the drill press.
9. Use the disc sander for final shaping of irregular shaped parts.
10. Belt sand all the flat surfaces as needed.
11. Assemble the parts.
12. Sand and finish the project.

Designing

Imagination is an absolute necessity in designing children's wooden toys. Without it the craftsman may encounter some difficulties in creating interesting products. Ideas and imagination can be developed by observing what is already available in stores. By observing commercially made toys, the craftsman can develop his own interpretation of what children will enjoy playing with in the home. Observing automobiles, trucks, boats, tractors, farm equipment and many other objects can also be helpful in producing ideas for wooden toys.

Making sketches of toy ideas while observing children at play can be very beneficial, too. These simple sketches can be a valuable resource in the home workshop. For example, a twig in the hands of a child can turn into a battleship, a ray gun, a space ship with a peculiar shape never thought of before, a troop of soldiers, and much more. It is at the time of observation that your sketch pad can

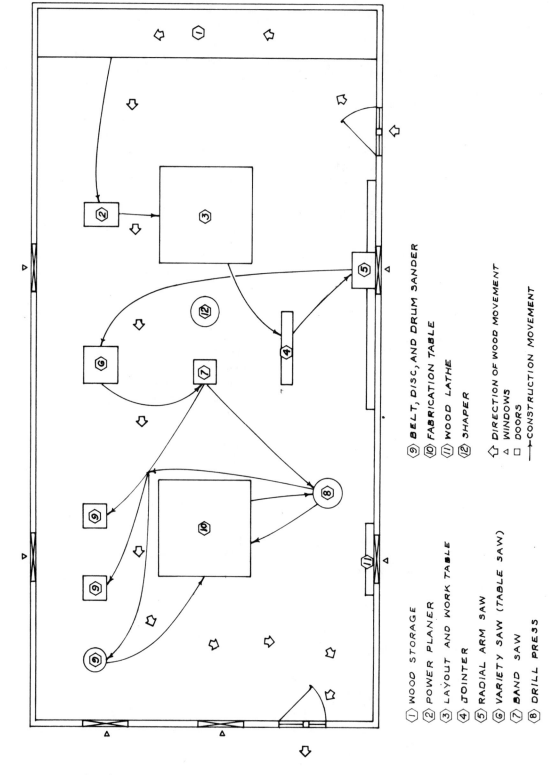

Figure I–1 Floor plan of wood shop.

1. WOOD STORAGE
2. POWER PLANER
3. LAYOUT AND WORK TABLE
4. JOINTER
5. RADIAL ARM SAW
6. VARIETY SAW (TABLE SAW)
7. BAND SAW
8. DRILL PRESS
9. BELT, DISC, AND DRUM SANDER
10. FABRICATION TABLE
11. WOOD LATHE
12. SHAPER

⇨ DIRECTION OF WOOD MOVEMENT
△ WINDOWS
☐ DOORS
→ CONSTRUCTION MOVEMENT

be used to advantage. Children's ideas are wild and interesting. They can be fun to interpret. It is wise to develop your ability to draw, at least to a small degree, and to take the time to develop your original ideas for toys.

Construction Drawings

After making a sketch, it is a good idea to refine your ideas by means of an orthographic (straight-on view, including width, height, and thickness) or isometric (three-dimensional) drawing. The drawings in this text are examples of what the craftsman can do himself. A catalog of working drawings are useful and will save a great deal of time. The drawings should include accurate and complete dimensions.

The simplest form of orthographic drawing includes three major views of the toys and parts. These three views are the top, side, and front. Solid lines represent visible edges; dashed lines represent concealed cuts or edges (what you would see if you had x-ray vision). Occasionally a fourth and fifth view is required to make the drawing easier to understand. Additional clarification can be provided via three-dimensional views. Isometric views will add depth to the drawings, if you wish to take the time to do them.

The plans for the wooden toys presented in this book were originally drawn to full scale, 1″ to 1″, on 17″ x 22″ mechanical drawing paper. They are reduced to fit the pages of this book, so that each drawing is proportional in relation to the redrawn, full scale plan. However, the dimensions shown in the drawing are "full scale" dimensions. You will want to redraw all patterns to full scale, using the indicated dimensions. A full-scale drawing will enable you to check each cut by superimposing it on the drawing. This eliminates many a costly mistake. After checking the cut, you can set your power tools for production work.

There are four basic reasons for developing complete drawings in the home workshop: 1) it helps increase shop efficiency; 2) it helps eliminate costly mistakes; 3) it helps improve the quality of the product; and 4) it provides a record of new ideas and new products that will prove useful to you in the future.

Before beginning construction of the toys in this book, study the drawings carefully. Remember that solid lines represent visible edges and dashed lines indicate "hidden" edges. If you understand how the parts are to be constructed and assembled, it will save you time and mistakes. In fact, a skilled craftsman should be able to study the drawings and construct each toy without being concerned with the step-by-step instructions.

The typical tools and supplies used to produce the drawings in this text are listed below.

1. Pencils and pens (2H, 3H, inking pen).
2. Drafting table (homemade).
3. Drafting board (size is optional).
4. "T" square
5. Mechanical drawing and drafting set.
6. Angles (30–60 degree, 45 degree).
7. Templates (circle templates, ellipse templates, lettering guides).

8. Sketch pad.
9. Mechanical drawing paper (17" x 22").

Patterns

After completing the orthographic and or isometric drawings, you are ready to make patterns for the toy. Patterns are made of hardwood, plate aluminum, or plastic. The choice of material depends upon what is available and personal preference. The patterns are used to trace toy parts onto the woodstock. They save time and wood, and they help increase efficiency in the shop. A complete set of properly labeled patterns will save many hours of labor and reduce confusion in the shop. Although patterns are more often used in commercial production, the hobbyist will also find them useful.

In the construction of Deno the Dino, Figure 26–1, for example, seven patterns were used. They include head and neck pattern, body side pattern, tail pattern, wheel pattern, inner brace pattern, cam wheel pattern, and peg nut pattern. If you desire, you might design the wheel patterns to fit more than one toy.

All patterns, including aluminum ones, can be cut and shaped on the shop equipment listed in the tool section. Aluminum plate is usually softer than the blades on the band saw, arm saw, and table saw, and you should have little trouble in cutting aluminum patterns with your shop equipment. I have made patterns from all three materials and have used them successfully in toy making.

Milling and Laying Out Woodstock

With the aid of patterns, tape measure, pencil, and combination square, you can determine how many board feet of hardwood to mill for the construction of a toy. After milling, the woodstock should be laid out on a work table for tracing and penciling of the toy parts. If additional wood is needed to complete a project, it should be milled at this time. When penciling the patterns on the hardwood, be sure to allow for saw cuts and blemishes. By carefully laying out the project this way, you will be able to tell exactly if you have the correct amount of hardwood for the project.

If you are filling an order for a large number of the same toy, it is best to complete the entire order before starting another project. By doing so, you will save time and will not have to reset the power tool equipment. Before going into full production, check each piece by superimposing each cut part over its drawing.

Gluing and Doweling

The assembly of many of the projects in this book requires parts to be joined by gluing and doweling. The dowels act as pegs to help align and hold the parts together. The general procedure is as follows:

1. Use $\frac{1}{4}''$ dowel pegs cut about $\frac{1}{4}''$ longer than needed for butt joint support.
2. Slightly taper the ends of all dowels and wheel axles so they can be tapped easily into the dowel holes.

3. Flatten one side of all dowels at each end ($\frac{1}{2}''$ up from the ends) so that excess glue can escape and so that the wood will not split when the dowel is tapped in place.
4. To avoid slipping and misalignment when gluing the joints, first clamp the parts to be joined together and drill the dowel holes. Remove the clamps and apply glue to the surfaces. Then tap the dowels in place and apply clamping pressure to the joint.
5. Remove all excess glue.
6. Allow glue to dry between assembly stages.
7. After the glue has dried, the excess dowel is sanded flush with the surface on the belt sander.

Marketing

Retail outlets for wooden toys vary greatly. Drug stores, grocery stores, hardware stores, furniture stores, automotive parts stores, toy stores, gift stores and craft stores are all possible sources of sales. You must take it upon yourself to develop your own market outlets. This takes time and continued effort. The quality and price of your product, plus your politeness to retailers, determines whether or not your product sells. You should also have simple but attractive packaging available for your toys.

Another possible source of sales is to develop a specific wooden toy for a particular store or company. The woodworker might find this task profitable as well as enjoyable.

Before taking orders, be aware of how your product is going to be presented to the public. The display should be decorative, eye catching, and placed so as to show off the qualities of each toy. This can be done if the retail owner will allow you a special section in the store to display the toys. A bright contrasting background will usually draw the attention of people in the store to the display.

As was stated earlier in this text, imagination helps not only in toy creation but also in sales.

·1·
Rolls Royce

Figure 1–1

The luxury car of yesterday and today can now be owned by one and all with a little construction work.

PART	DIMENSIONS	QUANTITY
	(thickness x width x length)	
1. Engine	$1\frac{7}{16}$ x $1\frac{5}{8}$ x $4\frac{1}{4}$	1
2. Fender	$\frac{13}{16}$ x 2 x $9\frac{9}{16}$	2 (R & L)
3. Wheels	$\frac{13}{16}$ x 2 dia.	4
4. Cab Sides	$\frac{1}{2}$ x $1\frac{3}{4}$ x $3\frac{1}{2}$	2
5. Cab Back	$\frac{1}{2}$ x 3 x $3\frac{1}{2}$	1
6. Cab Roof	$\frac{1}{2}$ x 3 x $3\frac{1}{4}$	1
7. Base	$\frac{13}{16}$ x 3 x $9\frac{1}{2}$	1
8. Radiator	$\frac{1}{2}$ x $1\frac{3}{4}$ x $1\frac{3}{4}$	1
9. Bumper	$\frac{1}{2}$ x $\frac{13}{16}$ x $4\frac{5}{8}$	1
10. Cab Parts	$\frac{1}{2}$ x $1\frac{3}{4}$ x 2	3
11. Cab Posts	$\frac{1}{4}$ dia. x $2\frac{1}{2}$	2
12. Head Lamps	$\frac{1}{2}$ dia. x 1	2
13. Head Lamp Posts	$\frac{1}{4}$ dia. x $1\frac{1}{2}$	2
14. Axles	$\frac{3}{8}$ dia. x 5	2

Construction

1. Redraw the Rolls Royce pattern pieces to full scale, using the dimensions shown in Figures 1–7 and 1–8.
2. Select the amount of clean, blemish-free hardwood stock needed to complete the project.
3. If not already milled, mill the rough 1″ lumber to $\frac{13}{16}$″ thickness.
4. If you do not have 2″ woodstock for the engine $\boxed{1}$, laminate enough $\frac{13}{16}$″ woodstock to obtain the desired thickness. Glue and clamp the woodstock together and allow to dry.
5. Prepare the production patterns as needed. One or two patterns of each item will suffice. Label each one for future use.
6. Place the woodstock on a work table and draw or trace all the toy parts on the milled woodstock. See Figure 1–2.
7. For easier handling, rough cut the woodstock into pieces approximately 8″ long or longer on the radial arm saw. See Figure 1–3. Be careful not to cut through any toy parts during this process.
8. Joint at least one edge of each piece of milled woodstock on the jointer. See Figure 1–4. Jointing gives a flat edge that permits square and parallel cuts to be made on the table saw and radial arm saw.
9. On the table saw or radial arm saw, cut the following parts to the exact rectangular dimensions listed previously. See the drawings for details. Some of these parts will be further shaped on the band saw and sanders.

$\boxed{1}$ Engine $\boxed{4}$ Cab Sides
$\boxed{2}$ Fenders $\boxed{5}$ Cab Back

|6| Cab Roof |9| Bumper
|7| Base |10| Cab Parts
|8| Radiator

10. Saw the following parts to $\frac{1}{2}''$ thickness on the table saw.
    |4| Cab Sides |8| Radiator
    |5| Cab Back |9| Bumper
    |6| Cab Roof |10| Cab Parts
11. Cut the following parts to size on the band saw, allowing a small amount of wood to remain outside the pencil lines. The final shaping and finishing is done on the disc, drum and belt sanders. See Figure 1–5.
    |2| Fenders |8| Radiator (angle only)
    |3| Wheels |14| Axles
12. Shape the following parts on the disc sander, belt sander, and drum sander.
    |2| Fenders |8| Radiator (angle only)
    |3| Wheels |14| Axles (taper ends slightly)
13. Drill $\frac{3}{8}''$ axle holes into the following parts. See drawings for details.
    |2| Fenders
    |3| Wheels
    |7| Base
14. Route out the fender wells |2| with the router. See drawings for details. You can route free hand, or you can build a template of wood or aluminum and route with the aid of a template guide.
15. Remove all sharp edges and corners with a router or sandpaper.
16. Belt sand all flat surfaces to remove the scratches and blemishes. Always sand with the grain of the wood, not across it, to prevent scratches.

Assembly

Note: For directions on gluing and doweling parts together, see the procedure described in the Introduction.
1. Glue and dowel the following parts together to form the cab. See drawings for details.
    |4| Cab Sides |10| Cab Parts
    |5| Cab Back |11| Cab Posts
    |6| Cab Roof
    Be sure to allow the sections to dry between assembly stages.
2. Glue and dowel the fenders |2| to the base |7|, being sure to line up the axle holes of the fenders with those of the base.
3. Glue and dowel the following sections and parts to the base |7|.
    Completed Cab Section
    |1| Engine |12| Head Lamps
    |8| Radiator |13| Head Lamp Posts
    |9| Bumper
4. Place the axles |14| into the axle holes of the base |7| and then glue the wheels |3| to the axles |14|. Drill the axle holes oversize if the axles do not turn freely.
5. Finish sanding the surface of the Rolls Royce with fine grit sand paper. This can be done by hand or with a small electric orbital sander.
6. Apply one or two coats of boiled linseed oil to finish the surface.

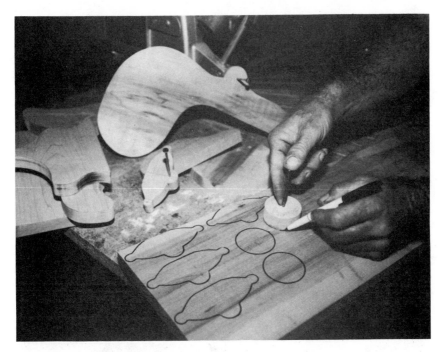

Figure 1–2   Drawing the toy parts on the milled woodstock.

Figure 1–3   Cutting the woodstock into rough lengths with a table saw.

Figure 1–4   Jointing an edge of a rough length of woodstock.

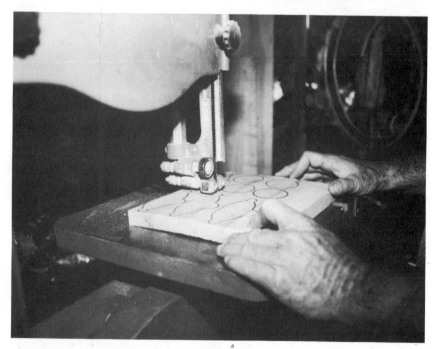

Figure 1–5   Cutting out toy parts on the band saw.

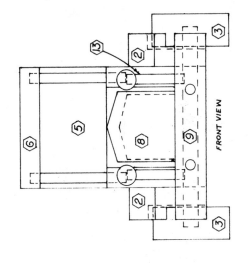

FRONT VIEW

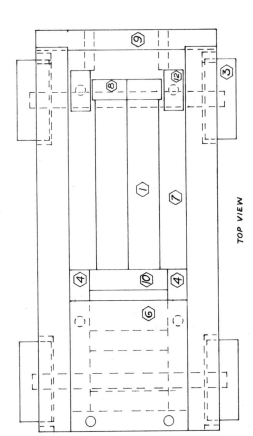

TOP VIEW

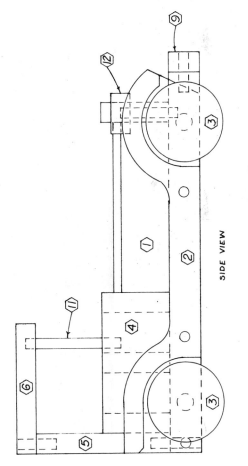

SIDE VIEW

Figure 1–6 Top, side, and front views of the Rolls Royce.

Figure 1–7 Rolls Royce patterns.

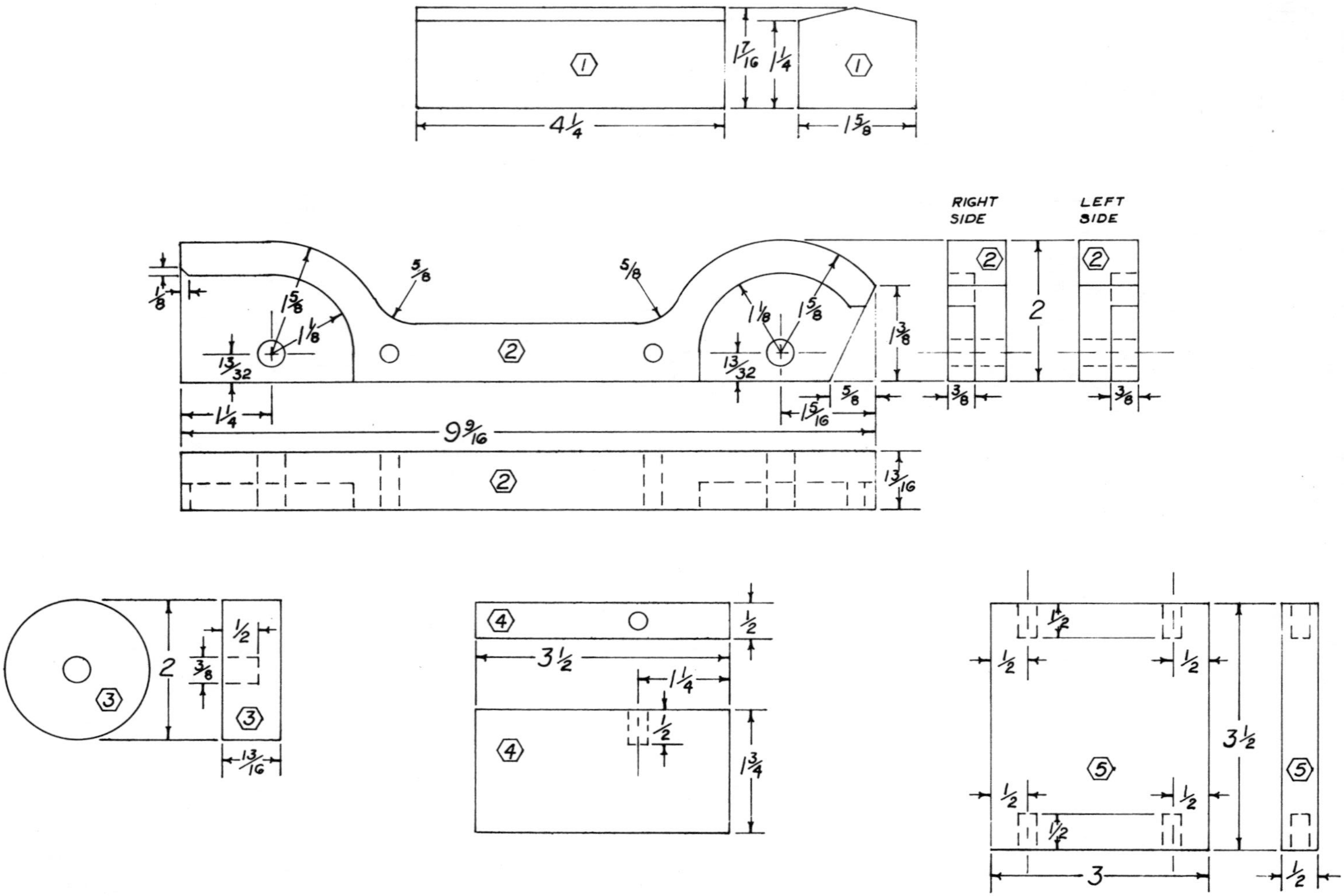

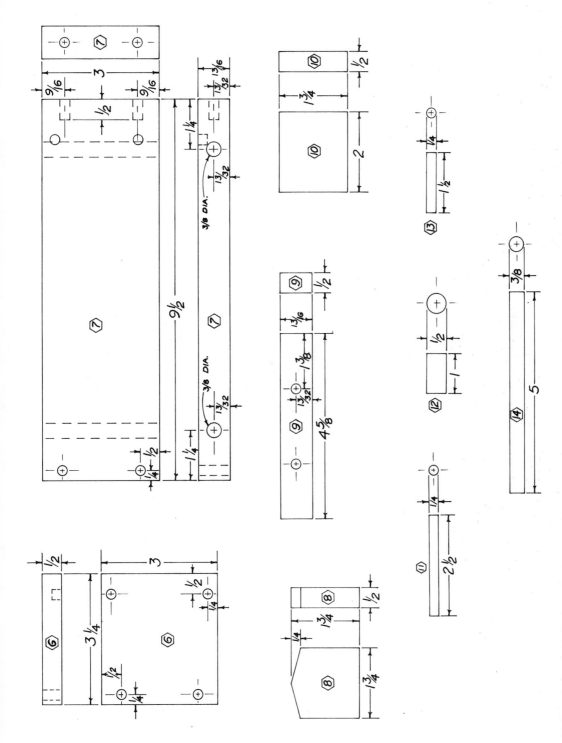

Figure 1-8 Rolls Royce patterns.

·2·
Peg Bus

Figure 2–1

The Peg Bus is simple in design and simple to construct.

PART	DIMENSIONS (thickness x width x length)	QUANTITY
1. Top	$\frac{13}{16}$ x 3 x 8	1
2. Posts	$\frac{3}{8}$ dia. x $4\frac{1}{8}$	4
3. Wheels	$\frac{13}{16}$ x $2\frac{1}{8}$ dia.	4
4. Base	$\frac{13}{16}$ x 3 x 8	1
5. Axles	$\frac{3}{8}$ dia. x $4\frac{1}{8}$	2

Construction

1. Redraw the Peg Bus pattern pieces to full scale, using the dimensions shown in Figure 2–3.
2. Select the amount of clean, blemish-free hardwood stock needed to complete the Peg Bus.
3. If not yet milled, mill the rough 1″ lumber to $\frac{13}{16}$″ thickness.
4. Prepare the production patterns as needed. Label each pattern for later use.
5. Place the woodstock on a work table and draw or trace all of the Peg Bus parts on the milled woodstock.
6. For easier handling, rough cut the woodstock to pieces approximately 8″ in length or longer on the radial arm saw. Be careful not to cut through a toy part during this process.
7. Joint the edges of the milled woodstock on the jointer. Jointing gives a flat edge that permits square and parallel cuts to be made on the table saw and radial arm saw.
8. On the table or radial arm saw, cut the following parts to the exact rectangular dimensions listed previously. See the drawings for details.
   - [1] Top
   - [4] Base
9. Cut the following parts out on the band saw, allowing a small amount of wood to remain beyond the pencil lines. The final shaping is done on the disc or belt sanders.
   - [2] Posts (cut to length)
   - [3] Wheels
10. Drill $\frac{3}{8}$″ axle holes into the wheels [3] and base [4]. See the drawings for details.
11. Drill 1″ peg people seat holes into the base [4] to depths indicated on the drawings. The size and position of the seat holes can vary. Make the peg people from 1″ doweling.
12. Drill $\frac{3}{8}$″ post holes into the top [1] and base [4]. See the drawings for details.
13. Disc sand the wheels [3] to exact size and shape.
14. Remove all sharp edges and corners with a router or sandpaper.
15. Belt sand all flat surfaces to remove scratches and blemishes. Be sure to sand with the wood grain, not across it, to prevent scratches.

Assembly

Note: For gluing and doweling parts together, see the procedure described in the Introduction.

1. Glue the posts 2 to the top 1 and the base 4.
2. Place the axles 5 into the base 4 axles holes, and then glue the wheels 3 to the axles 5.
3. Finish sanding the surface of the Peg Bus with fine grit sand paper.
4. Apply one or two coats of boiled linseed oil to finish the surface.

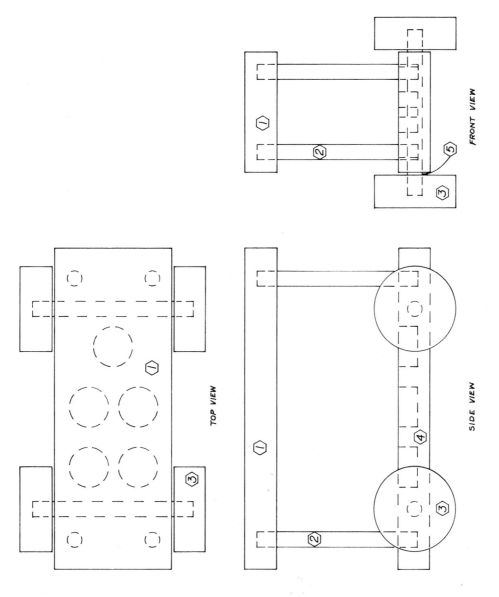

Figure 2-2   Top, side, and front views of the Peg Bus.

TOP VIEW

SIDE VIEW

FRONT VIEW

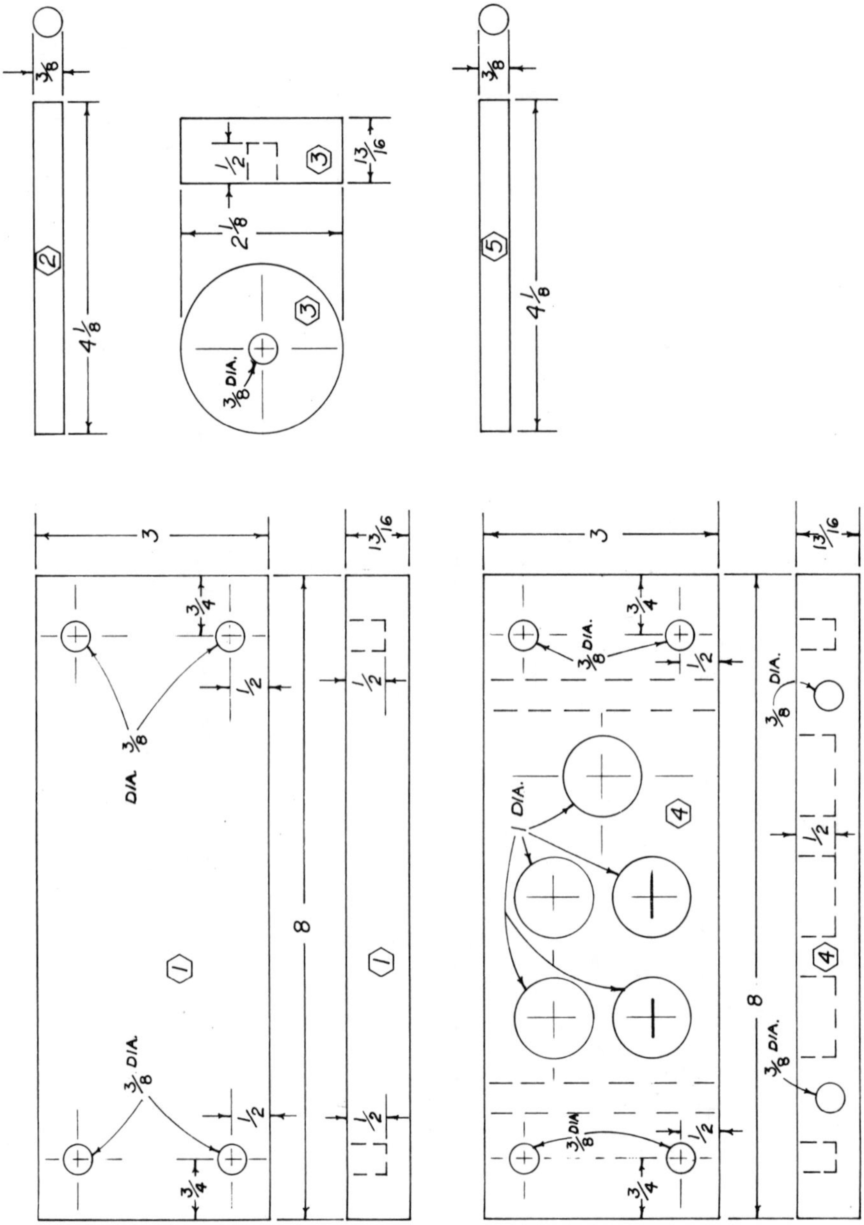

Figure 2–3   Peg Bus patterns.

·3·
Block Car

Figure 3–1

Even a small block of wood can be transformed
into a useful toy.

PART	DIMENSIONS (thickness x width x length)	QUANTITY
1. Car Body	$1\frac{7}{8}$ x $2\frac{1}{2}$ x $5\frac{3}{4}$	1
2. Wheel	$\frac{13}{16}$ x $1\frac{5}{8}$ dia.	4
3. Axle	$\frac{1}{4}$ dia. x $3\frac{3}{8}$	2

Construction

1. Redraw the Block Car patterns to full scale, using the dimensions shown in Figure 3–4.
2. Select the amount of clean, blemish-free hardwood stock needed to complete the Block Car.
3. If not already milled, mill the rough 1″ lumber to $\frac{13}{16}$″ thickness.
4. If you do not have 2″ woodstock for the car body, laminate enough $\frac{13}{16}$″ stock together to achieve the desired thickness. Glue and clamp the woodstock together and allow to dry.
5. Prepare the body ① pattern and wheel ② pattern if needed. Label each pattern for later use.
6. Place the woodstock on a work table and draw or trace the body ① and wheels ② on the milled woodstock.
7. For easier handling, rough cut the woodstock to pieces 8″ in length or longer on the radial arm saw. Be careful not to cut through a toy part during this process.
8. Joint the edges of the milled woodstock on the jointer. Jointing gives a flat edge that permits square and parallel cuts to be made on the table saw and radial arm saw.
9. On the table saw or radial arm saw, cut the car body ① to the exact dimensions listed previously.
10. Cut the following parts out on the band saw, allowing a small amount of excess wood to remain beyond the pencil lines. Final finish sanding and shaping will be done on the disc and belt sanders.
    ① Car Body
    ② Wheels
    ③ Axles
11. Drill $\frac{1}{4}$″ axle holes into the car body ① and wheels ②, using a floor model drill press and $\frac{1}{4}$″ speed bit or portable electric hand drill. Drill the axle holes slightly oversize if the axles will not turn freely.
12. Drill peg people seat holes into the car body ① as shown on the drawings. The seat holes can be whatever size you wish. Make the peg people from commercial dowelling.
13. Disc sand the car body ① and wheels ② to exact size and shape. Taper axles slightly on each end. This helps to prevent wheels from splitting when the axles are tapped into axle holes.

14. Remove all the sharp edges from the parts with a router or sand paper.
15. Belt sand the car body and wheels to remove scratches and blemishes. Be sure to sand with the wood grain, not across it, to prevent scratches.

Assembly

Note: For how to glue and dowel parts together, see the procedure described in the Introduction.

1. Place the axles ③ into the car body ① axle holes, and then glue the wheels ② to the axles ③. Drill the axle holes slightly oversize if the axles do not turn freely.
2. Finish sanding the surface of the Block Car with fine grit sand paper. This can be done by hand or with an electric orbital sander.
3. Apply one or two coats of boiled linseed oil to the surface of the Block Car.

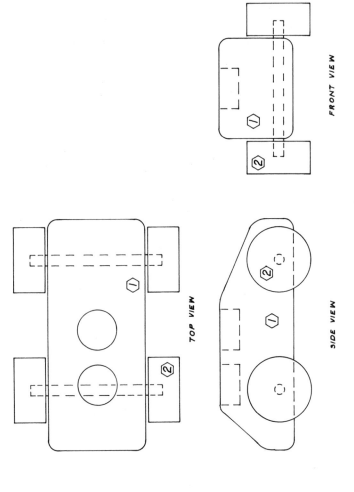

Figure 3-2 Top, side, and front views of the Block Car.

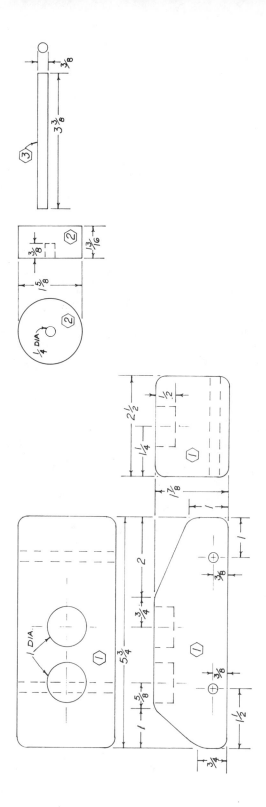

Figure 3–3 Block Car patterns.

·4·

Family Car

Figure 4–1

Every child wants to drive the family car, and this handsome
toy makes it possible.

PART	DIMENSIONS (thickness x width x length)	QUANTITY
1. Sides	$\frac{13}{16}$ x 3 x 7	2 (R & L)
2. Wheel	$\frac{13}{16}$ x $1\frac{1}{2}$ dia.	4
3. Base	$\frac{13}{16}$ x $2\frac{1}{4}$ x 7	1
4. Axle	$\frac{1}{4}$ dia. x $4\frac{3}{4}$	2

Construction

1. Redraw the Family Car pattern pieces to full scale, using the dimensions shown in Figure 4–3.
2. Select the amount of clean, blemish-free hardwood stock needed to complete the Family Car.
3. If not already milled, mill the rough 1″ hardwood stock to $\frac{13}{16}$″ thickness.
4. Prepare patterns if needed for production work. Label each pattern for shop use.
5. Place the woodstock on a work table and draw or trace the parts of the Family Car on the milled hardwood.
6. Rough cut the woodstock to pieces 8″ in length or longer on the radial arm saw. Do not cut through any toy parts during this process.
7. Joint the edges of the milled woodstock on the jointer. Jointing gives a flat edge that permits square and parallel cuts to be made on the table saw and radial arm saw.
8. On the table saw or radial arm saw, cut the following parts to the exact dimensions previously listed. The parts will be further shaped on the band saw or table saw.
   - ☐1 Sides
   - ☐3 Base
9. Drill $\frac{1}{4}$″ axle holes into the wheels ☐2 and base ☐3. Drill $1\frac{1}{4}$″ window holes into the sides ☐1. Drill 1″ peg people seat holes into the base ☐3. See drawings for details. A floor model drill press, $\frac{1}{4}$″ speed bit, 1″ speed bit, and $1\frac{1}{4}$″ circle saw will do the job. Drill the axle holes in the base ☐3 slightly oversize.
10. Cut the sides ☐1 and wheels ☐2 out on the band saw. Allow excess wood to remain beyond the pencil lines so that the final finish sanding can be done on the disc, belt, and drum sanders.
11. Cut the slanted cut of the sides ☐1 on the table saw. See the drawings for details.
12. Disc sand the following parts to shape on a disc sander.
    - ☐1 Sides
    - ☐2 Wheels
    - ☐3 Base (ends)
13. Shape the front concave curve of the sides ☐1 on the drum sander.
14. Remove all sharp edges and corners with the router or sandpaper.

15. Belt sand the following parts to remove scratches and blemishes, sanding with the grain of the wood, not against it.
    1. Sides
    2. Wheels
    3. Base

Assembly

Note: For how to glue and dowel parts together, see the procedure described in the Introduction.

1. Clamp the right and left sides 1 to the base 3 and then drill $\frac{1}{4}''$ dowel holes through the sides 1 and into the base 3. Align the axle holes before drilling the dowel holes.
2. After drilling the dowel holes, glue, dowel, and clamp the sides 1 to the base 3.
3. Place the axles 4 into the axle holes of the base 3 and sides 1 and then glue the wheels 2 to the axles 4.
4. Finish sanding the surface of the Family Car with fine grit sandpaper. Hand sand or use a small electric orbital sander.
5. Apply one or two coats of boiled linseed oil to the surface of the Family Car as a finish.

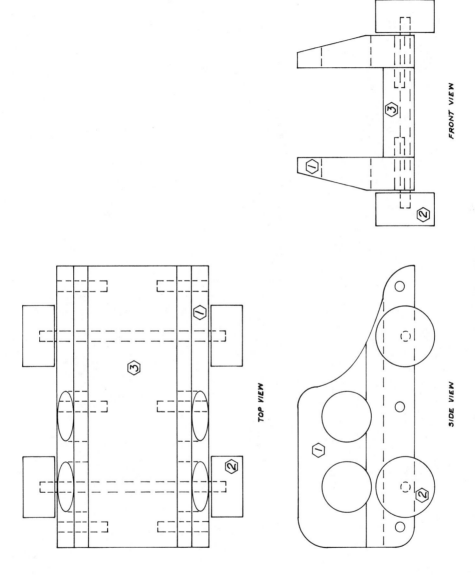

FRONT VIEW

TOP VIEW

SIDE VIEW

Figure 4–2   Top, side, and front views of the Family Car.

29

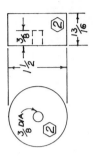

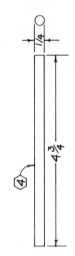

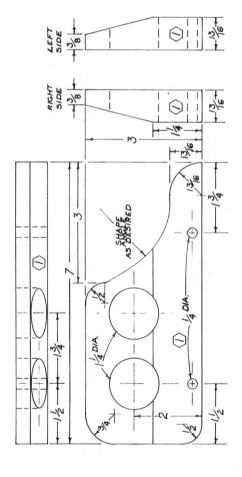

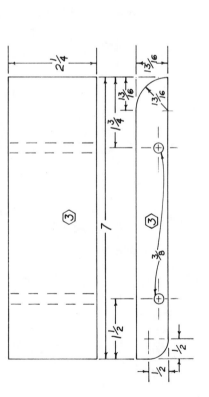

Figure 4–3   Family Car patterns.

30

·5·

Train Engine

Figure 5–1

The Train Engine has always been a delight to children.
You can vary the looks of the train by redesigning the engine
boiler 3 and the smoke stack 4.

PART	DIMENSIONS (thickness x width x length)	QUANTITY
1. Cab Roof	$\frac{13}{16}$ x $2\frac{1}{4}$ x 3	1
2. Stand	$\frac{13}{16}$ x $2\frac{1}{4}$ x 3	1
3. Boiler	$1\frac{3}{4}$ dia. x $5\frac{3}{4}$	1
4. Smoke Stack	2 dia. x $3\frac{1}{4}$	1
5. Seat	$\frac{13}{16}$ x 1 x $2\frac{1}{4}$	1
6. Wheel	$\frac{13}{16}$ x 2 dia.	6
7. Base	$\frac{13}{16}$ x $2\frac{1}{4}$ x $7\frac{1}{2}$	1
8. Axle	$\frac{3}{8}$ dia. x $3\frac{1}{4}$	3

Construction

1. Redraw the Train Engine patterns to full scale, using the dimensions shown on Figure 5–3.
2. Select the amount of clean, blemish-free hardwood stock needed to complete the Train Engine.
3. If not already milled, mill the rough 1″ hardwood stock to $\frac{13}{16}$″ thickness.
4. If 2″ woodstock is not available, glue enough $\frac{13}{16}$″ stock together to form the desired thicknesses for the boiler ③ and smoke stack ④.
5. Prepare patterns if needed for production work. Label each pattern for shop use.
6. Place the woodstock on a work table and draw or trace the parts of the Train Engine on the milled hardwood.
7. Rough cut the woodstock to pieces 8″ long or longer on the radial arm saw, being careful not to cut through any toy parts.
8. Joint the edges of the milled woodstock on the jointer to provide a flat edge to guide subsequent cuts on the table saw and radial arm saw.
9. On the table saw or radial arm saw, cut the following parts to the exact dimensions listed previously.
   ① Roof   ④ Smoke Stack
   ② Stand   ⑤ Seat
   ③ Boiler   ⑦ Base
10. Cut the slanted front end of the base ⑦ on the table saw. See drawings for details.
11. Cut the following parts out on the band saw. Allow excess wood to remain beyond the pencil lines so that the final finish sanding can be done on the disc or belt sanders.
    ⑥ Wheels
    ⑧ Axles (cut to length)
12. Disc sand the wheels ⑥ and axles ⑧ to size and shape. Taper the ends of the axles slightly so that they will be easier to tap into the wheel axle holes.
13. Drill $\frac{3}{8}$″ axle holes into the wheels ⑥ and base ⑦, using a floor model drill

press or electric hand drill and $\frac{3}{8}''$ speed bit. See the drawings for details. Drill the axle holes slightly oversize if they do not turn freely.

14. Shape the boiler ③ and smoke stack ④ on the wood lathe. See the drawings for details.

15. Sand a 1″ wide flat surface along the length of the boiler ③ on the belt sander. The flat surface forms the butt joint between the boiler ③ and the base ⑦.

16. Drill a $\frac{3}{8}''$ smoke stack hole into the engine boiler ③. See drawings for details.

17. Remove all of the sharp edges and corners with a router or with sandpaper.

18. Belt sand the following parts to remove scratches and blemishes, sanding with the grain, not across it.
    ① Cab Roof   ⑥ Wheels
    ② Stand   ⑦ Base
    ⑤ Seat

Assembly

Note: For how to glue and dowel parts together, see the procedure described in the Introduction.

1. Glue and dowel the following parts together to form the body of the train engine.
    ① Cab Roof   ⑤ Seat
    ② Stand   ⑦ Base

2. Glue and dowel the boiler ③ to the base ⑦. Clamp the parts together and allow to dry.

3. Glue the smoke stack ④ to the boiler ③.

4. Place the axles ⑧ into the axle holes of the base ⑦ and then glue the wheels ⑧ to the axles ⑧.

5. Finish sanding the entire surface of the train engine with medium or fine grit sandpaper.

6. To finish the surface, apply one or two coats of boiled linseed oil.

Figure 5–2 Top, side, and front views of the Train Engine.

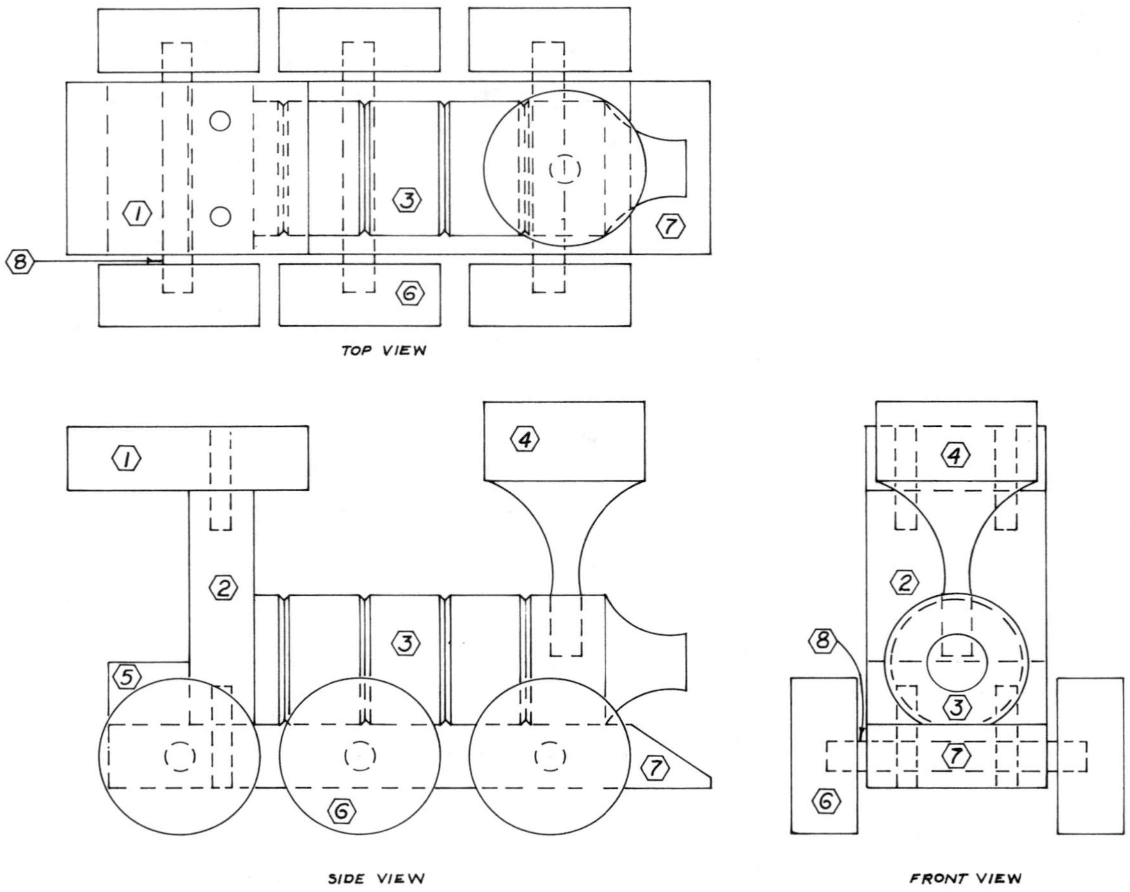

TOP VIEW

SIDE VIEW

FRONT VIEW

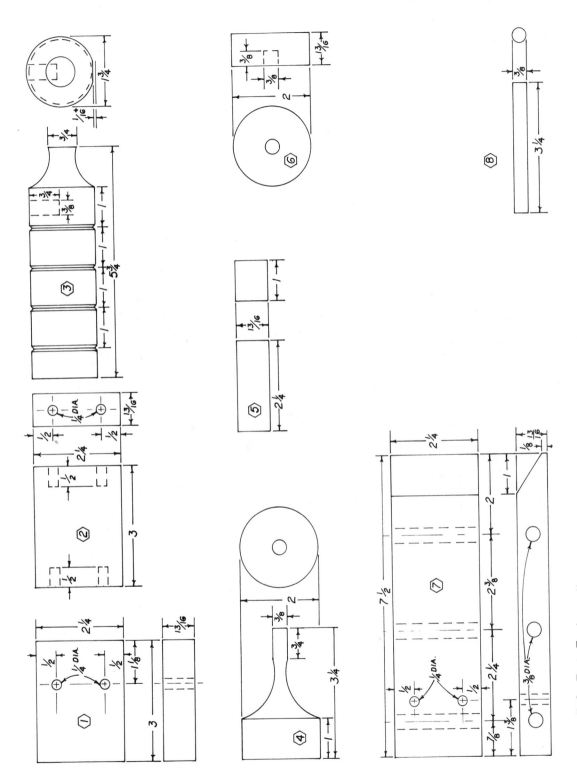

Figure 5-3   Train Engine patterns.

·6·
Tic Tac Toe

Figure 6–1

An old game becomes a new challenge when played on one of the beautiful hardwoods. The board can be designed to any shape you want: ours is round.

PART	DIMENSIONS	QUANTITY
1. Game Board	$\frac{13}{16}$ thick x $8\frac{1}{4}$ dia.	1

Game Instructions

When your board is completed, you'll need 5 red and 5 white marbles, and one blue marble, in order to play.

The object of the game is to place three marbles in a horizontal, vertical or diagonal row without having your opponent block your move. A tie game goes to the fictitious third player called "The Cat." The eleventh marble on the board determines who moves first and should alternate between players at the end of each game.

Construction

1. Redraw the game board pattern to full scale, using the dimensions shown on Figure 6–2.
2. Select the amount of clean, blemish-free hardwood needed to complete the game board.
3. If not already milled, mill the rough 1″ hardwood stock to $\frac{13}{16}″$ thickness.
4. Prepare a pattern of the game board if needed for production work. Label the pattern for later use in the shop.
5. Place the woodstock on a work table and draw or trace the game board on the milled hardwood.
6. Rough cut the woodstock to easy-to-handle lengths on the radial arm saw, being careful not to cut through the tracing of the game board.
7. Cut the game board out on the band saw, cutting slightly outside the pencil lines so that the final finish sanding can be done on the disc or belt sanders.
8. Drill $\frac{1}{2}″$ game board holes to a depth of $\frac{1}{4}″$ to $\frac{3}{8}″$. See the drawings for details. The size of the game board holes can vary depending upon the size of marbles to be used to play the game.
9. Disc sand the game board to the desired shape.
10. Rout off all sharp edges.
11. Sand the game board surface with medium grit or fine grit sand paper. Sand in the direction of the wood grain, not across it, to prevent scratches. An electric hand orbital sander will do an adequate job.
12. Apply boiled linseed oil to the surfaces of the game board as a final finish.

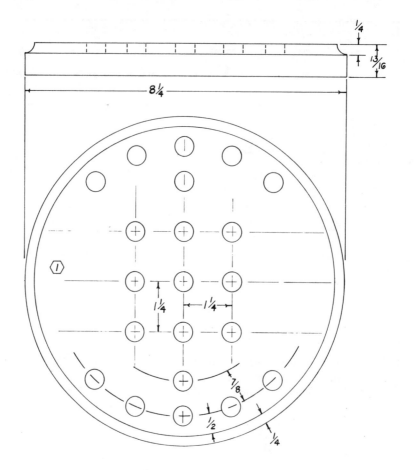

Figure 6–2   Tic Tac Toe pattern.

·7·
Rattle

Figure 7–1

The rattle is often one of the first toys a child enjoys.
Not only does it make a noise, but it also intrigues the child
because the clapper is visible in its little cage.

PART	DIMENSIONS (thickness x length)	QUANTITY
1. Top and Bottom	$\frac{13}{16}$ x $3\frac{1}{4}$ dia.	1 each
2. Dowel Post	$\frac{3}{8}$ dia. x $3\frac{3}{8}$	8
3. Clapper	$\frac{13}{16}$ x $1\frac{1}{2}$ dia.	1

Construction

1. Redraw the Rattle patterns to full scale, using the dimensions shown in Figure 7–2.
2. Select the amount of clean, blemish-free hardwood stock needed to complete the Rattle.
3. If required, mill the rough 1″ hardwood stock to $\frac{13}{16}$″ thickness.
4. Place the milled woodstock on a worktable and draw or trace the rattle parts onto it.
5. Rough cut the woodstock to easy-to-handle lengths on the radial arm saw, being careful not to cut through any parts of the toy.
6. Cut the following parts out on the band saw, cutting slightly outside the pencil lines so that final shaping and sanding can be done on the disc or belt sanders.
   - 1 Top and Bottom
   - 2 Posts
   - 3 Clapper
7. Drill $\frac{3}{8}$″ post holes into the top and bottom 1 to $\frac{3}{8}$″ depth as shown on the drawings. Drill the center hole for the clapper 3. A floor model drill press or electric hand drill and $\frac{3}{8}$″ speed bit will do the job.
8. Shape the following parts on the disc sander.
   - 1 Top and Bottom
   - 2 Posts
   - 3 Clapper

   Taper the ends of the posts and flatten one side about $\frac{1}{2}$″ up from each end. This will allow the excess glue to escape and prevent the wood from splitting when the posts are tapped in place.
9. Rout off all of the sharp edges on each part.
10. Sand the flat surfaces with medium grit or fine grit sand paper. Sand in the direction of the wood grain, not across it, to prevent scratches.

Assembly

1. Glue the eight $\frac{3}{8}$″ posts 2 to the top 1.
2. Place the clapper 3 inside the circle of $\frac{3}{8}$″ dowel posts 2. Tap the dowel posts in place with a hammer.
3. Glue the bottom side 1 to the ring of $\frac{3}{8}$″ dowel posts 2.
4. Finish sanding the surfaces of the top and bottom sides 1, using medium or fine grit sandpaper.
5. Apply one or two coats of boiled linseed oil to finish the surface.

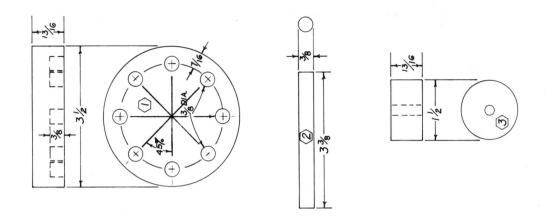

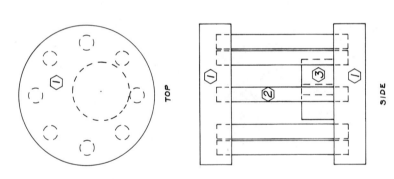

TOP

SIDE

Figure 7-2 Top and side views and Rattle patterns.

·8·
Tractor

Figure 8–1

The tractor is the symbol of the modern day farmer
and is a must for any child who wants to go into farming on
mom's livingroom rug.

PART	DIMENSIONS (thickness x width x length)	QUANTITY
1. Cab Roof	$\frac{13}{16}$ x $2\frac{3}{4}$ x 3	1
2. Cab Post	$\frac{3}{8}$ dia. x $4\frac{3}{16}$	4
3. Exhaust Pipe	$\frac{3}{8}$ dia. x 2	1
4. Tractor Body	$2\frac{3}{4}$ x 4 x $6\frac{3}{4}$	1
5. Rear Wheel	$\frac{13}{16}$ x 5 dia.	2
6. Front Wheel	$\frac{13}{16}$ x $2\frac{3}{8}$ dia.	2
7. Rear Axle	$\frac{3}{8}$ dia. x $3\frac{3}{4}$	1
8. Front Axle	$\frac{3}{8}$ dia. x $2\frac{3}{4}$	1

Construction

1. Redraw the tractor patterns to full scale, using the dimensions shown in Figure 8–3.
2. Select the amount of clean, blemish-free hardwood stock needed to complete the tractor.
3. If not already milled, mill the rough 1″ woodstock to $\frac{13}{16}$″ thickness.
4. If you do not have 2″ woodstock for the tractor body ④, laminate enough 1″ woodstock to obtain the desired thickness. Glue and clamp the woodstock together and allow to dry.
5. Prepare the production patterns as needed. Label each one for later use.
6. Place the milled woodstock on a worktable and draw or trace all of the tractor parts on to it.
7. For easier handling, cut the wood into pieces approximately 8″ long or longer on the radial arm saw. Be careful not to cut through any toy parts during this process.
8. Joint the edges of the milled woodstock on the jointer. This gives a flat edge so that square and parallel cuts can be made on the table saw and radial arm saw.
9. On the table saw or radial arm saw, cut the following parts to the exact rectangular dimensions listed previously.
   ① Cab Roof
   ④ Tractor Body
10. Cut the following parts out on the band saw.
   ② Cab Posts
   ③ Exhaust Pipe
   ⑤ Rear Wheels
   ⑥ Front Wheels
   ⑦ Rear Axle
   ⑧ Front Axle
   Leave a small amount of wood to remain outside the pencil lines so that final finish sanding can be done on the disc or belt sanders.
11. Disc sand the following parts to size and shape.
   ② Cab Posts
   ③ Exhaust Pipe
   ⑤ Rear Wheels
   ⑥ Front Wheels
   ⑦ Rear Axle
   ⑧ Front Axle

Slightly taper the ends of the cab posts, exhaust pipe, and axles. Flatten one side of the dowelling about $\frac{1}{2}''$ up from each end. This will allow the excess glue to escape and prevent the wood from splitting when the dowels are tapped into the holes.

12. Make sure that the sides of the tractor body [4] are parallel with one another. It may be necessary to joint one edge or side of the tractor body [4] before shaping it on the table saw.

13. Cut and shape the tractor body [4] on the table saw. The recesses of the tractor body [4] can be shaped on the table saw and dado head or cut on the band saw, whichever is most convenient. See drawings for dimensions and details.

14. Drill $\frac{3}{8}''$ holes into the following parts.
    [1] Cab Roof   [5] Rear Wheel
    [4] Tractor Body   [6] Front Wheel
    See the blueprints for details. The peg people seat hole may be drilled to whatever size you want.

15. Remove all sharp edges with a router or sandpaper.

16. Belt sand all of the flat surfaces to remove scratches and blemishes. Always sand with the woodgrain to prevent scratches.

Assembly

Note: For how to glue and dowel parts together, see the procedure described in the Introduction.

1. Glue the cab posts [2] to the tractor body [4] and the cab roof [1].
2. Place the rear axle [7] and front axle [8] into the the tractor body [4] (axle housing). Then glue the wheels [5] and [6] to the axles [7] and [8].
3. Glue the exhaust pipe [3] into the hole at the front of the tractor.
4. Finish sanding the tractor with medium grit and fine grit sandpaper.
5. Apply one or two coats of boiled linseed oil to the surface of the tractor.

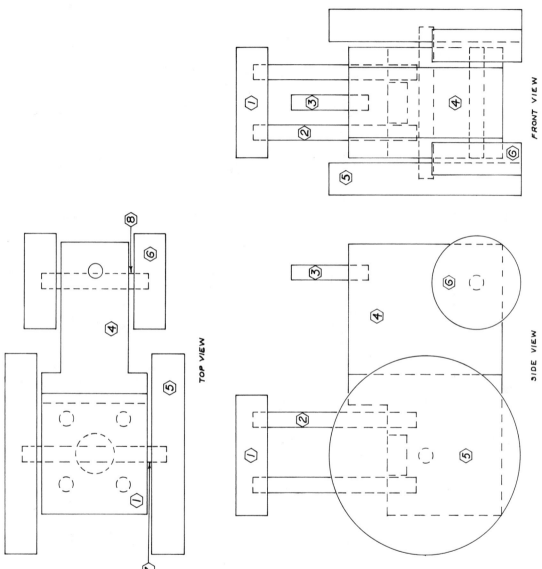

TOP VIEW

FRONT VIEW

SIDE VIEW

Figure 8–2 Top, side, and front views of the Tractor.

45

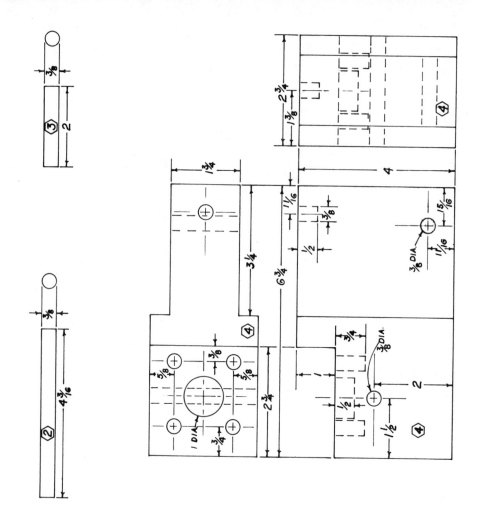

Figure 8–3 Tractor patterns.

46

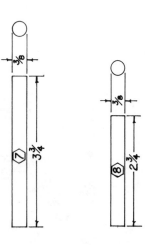

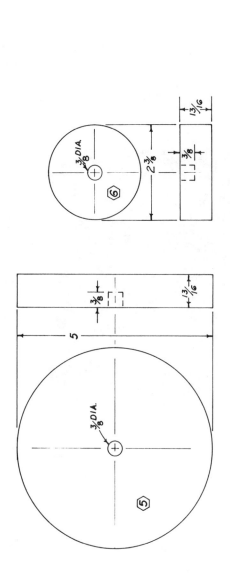

Figure 8–4 Tractor patterns.

·9·

Ladder Truck

Figure 9–1

The Ladder Truck can be used on many rescue missions or
climbing expeditions in the livingroom or back yard.
The three peg people that operate the truck can be made from
1″ dowel or shaped as desired from other woodstock.

PART	DIMENSIONS (thickness x width x length)	QUANTITY
1. Cab Roof	$\frac{13}{16}$ x 3 x 4	1
2. Cab Post	$\frac{3}{8}$ dia. x $4\frac{1}{8}$	4
3. Ladder Base	$1\frac{3}{8}$ x $1\frac{5}{8}$ x 3	1
4. Base	$\frac{13}{16}$ x 3 x 8	1
5. Wheel	$\frac{13}{16}$ x $2\frac{3}{8}$ dia.	4
6. Axle	$\frac{3}{8}$ dia. x $4\frac{1}{4}$	2
7. Ladder Rail	$\frac{1}{2}$ x $\frac{7}{8}$ x 9	9
8. Ladder Rung	$\frac{1}{4}$ dia. x $2\frac{1}{8}$	7
9. Ladder Peg Top	$\frac{5}{8}$ x 1 dia.	1
10. Ladder Peg	$\frac{1}{4}$ dia. x $3\frac{1}{4}$	1

Construction

1. Redraw the Ladder Truck pattern pieces to full scale, using the dimensions shown in Figure 9–3.
2. Select the amount of clean, blemish-free hardwood stock needed to complete the Ladder Truck.
3. If not already milled, mill the rough 1″ woodstock to $\frac{13}{16}$″ thickness.
4. If you do not have 2″ woodstock for the ladder base ③, laminate enough 1″ woodstock to obtain the desired thickness. Glue and clamp the woodstock together and allow to dry.
5. Prepare the production patterns as needed. Label each pattern for later use.
6. Place the milled woodstock on a worktable and draw or trace all of the toy parts on to it.
7. For easier handling, cut the hardwood into pieces approximately 8″ long or longer on the radial arm saw. Be careful not to cut through any toy parts during this process.
8. Joint the edges of the milled woodstock on the jointer to provide a flat edge to guide future cuts on the table saw and radial arm saw.
9. On the table saw or radial arm saw, cut the following parts to the exact rectangular dimensions listed previously.
   ① Cab Top ④ Base
   ③ Ladder Base ⑦ Ladder Rails
10. Cut the following parts on the band saw.
   ② Cab Posts ⑥ Axles
   ⑤ Wheels ⑧ Ladder Rungs
   Allow a small amount of wood to remain outside the pencil lines so that the final shaping and finish sanding can be done on the disc or belt sanders.
11. Disc sand the following parts to size and shape.
   ② Cab Posts ⑥ Axles
   ⑤ Wheels ⑧ Ladder Rungs

Slightly taper the ends of the cab posts, axles, and ladder rungs. Then flatten one side of the dowel about $\frac{1}{2}''$ up from each end. This will allow the excess glue to escape and prevent the wood from splitting when the dowels are tapped into place.

12. Drill $\frac{3}{8}''$ holes into the following parts. See drawings for details.
    1 Cab Roof (post holes)
    4 Base (post holes and axle holes)
    5 Wheels (axle holes)
13. Drill 1" peg people seat holes into the base 4. See drawings for details.
14. Drill $\frac{1}{4}''$ holes into the ladder base 3 and the ladder rails 7. See the blueprints for details.
15. Remove all sharp edges and corners with the router or sandpaper.
16. Belt sand all of the flat surfaces to a smooth finish. Always sand with the woodgrain to prevent scratches.

Assembly

Note: For how to glue and dowel parts together, see the procedure described in the Introduction.
1. Glue the cab posts 2 to the cab top 1 and base 4.
2. Glue the ladder base 3 to the base 4.
3. Place the axles 6 in the axle holes of the base 4 and then glue the wheels 5 to the axles 6.
4. Glue the ladder rungs 8 to the two ladder rails 7.
5. Finish sanding the surface as needed to remove scratches and blemishes. Use medium fine grit sandpaper.

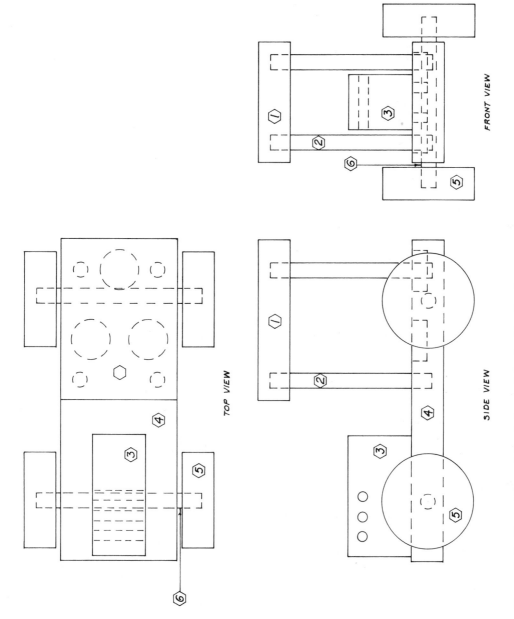

TOP VIEW

SIDE VIEW

FRONT VIEW

Figure 9–2   Top, side, and front views of the Ladder Truck.

51

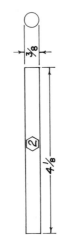

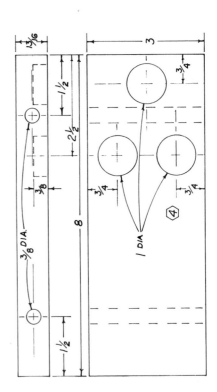

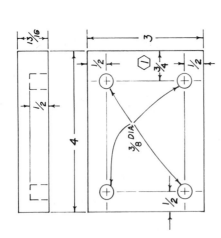

Figure 9–3 Ladder Truck patterns.

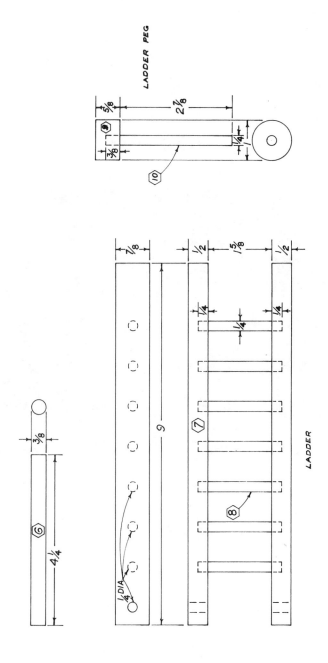

Figure 9–4 Ladder Truck patterns.

53

·10·
Airplane

Figure 10–1

A toy airplane makes imaginary flight possible for every child.
This airplane is simple in design and easy to build.

PART	DIMENSIONS (thickness x width x length)	QUANTITY
1. Airplane Body	$1\frac{11}{16}$ x 2 x 10	1
2. Wing	$\frac{3}{8}$ x 2 x $9\frac{1}{2}$	1
3. Rudder	$\frac{3}{8}$ x 2 x 3	1
4. Elevator	$\frac{3}{8}$ x $1\frac{1}{2}$ x 4	1
5. Wheel	$\frac{13}{16}$ x $1\frac{1}{2}$ dia.	1
6. Front Stabilizer	$\frac{3}{8}$ dia. x $1\frac{1}{8}$	1

Construction

1. Redraw the Airplane pattern pieces to full scale, using the dimensions shown in Figure 10–3.
2. Select the amount of clean, blemish-free hardwood needed to complete the Airplane.
3. If not already milled, mill the rough 1″ woodstock to $\frac{13}{16}$″ thickness.
4. If 2″ woodstock is not available for the airplane body [1], laminate enough $\frac{13}{16}$″ stock together to achieve the desired thickness. Glue and clamp the woodstock together and allow to dry.
5. Prepare the production patterns as needed. Label each pattern for later use.
6. Place the milled woodstock on a worktable and draw or trace all of the Airplane parts onto it.
7. For easier handling, cut the hardwood into pieces approximately 8″ long on the radial arm saw. Do not cut through any toy parts during this process.
8. To provide a straight edge to guide future cuts on each piece, joint the edges of the milled woodstock on the jointer.
9. On the table saw or radial arm saw, cut the following parts to the exact rectangular dimensions listed previously.
   [1] Airplane Body   [3] Rudder
   [2] Wing   [4] Elevator
10. Re-saw the following parts to the desired thickness on the table saw. See drawings for details.
    [2] Wing
    [3] Rudder
    [4] Elevator
11. Cut the following parts to shape on the band saw. (See step 14.)
    [1] Airplane Body   [4] Elevator
    [2] Wing   [5] Wheel
    [3] Rudder   [6] Stabilizer

    Do not cut into the pencil lines. Allow a small amount of wood to remain outside the lines so that the final shaping can be done on the disc or belt sanders.

12. Disc sand the following parts to shape.
    - 1 Airplane Body (shape the nose and tail)
    - 2 Wing
    - 3 Rudder
    - 4 Elevator
    - 5 Wheel
    - 6 Stabilizer
13. Drill one $\frac{3}{8}''$ hole for the stabilizer and six $\frac{5}{8}''$ holes for the windows into the airplane body 1. See drawings for details.
14. Cut the wing slot into the airplane body 1 on the table saw or radial arm saw with the aid of the dado head. This operation can be done before shaping the airplane body 1 on the band saw or shaping on the disc sander. See drawings for details.
15. Cut the rudder slot into the tail section of the airplane body 1 with the aid of a router and $\frac{3}{8}''$ straight shank router bit.
16. Cut the wheel into two equal halves on the band saw. The two halves will be glued to the underside of the wing 2 during the assembly steps.
17. Remove all sharp edges and corners.
18. Belt sand all of the flat surfaces to remove scratches and blemishes. Always sand with the grain of the wood to prevent scratches.

Assembly
1. Glue the wing 2 to the airplane body 1.
2. Glue the rudder 3 into the rudder slot at the tail section of the airplane body 1.
3. Glue the elevator 4 to the rudder 3.
4. Glue the wheel halves 5 to the wing 2.
5. Glue the stabilizer 6 to the airplane body 1.
6. Finish sand the airplane body with medium or fine grit sandpaper.
7. Apply one or two coats of boiled linseed oil to the surface of the airplane.

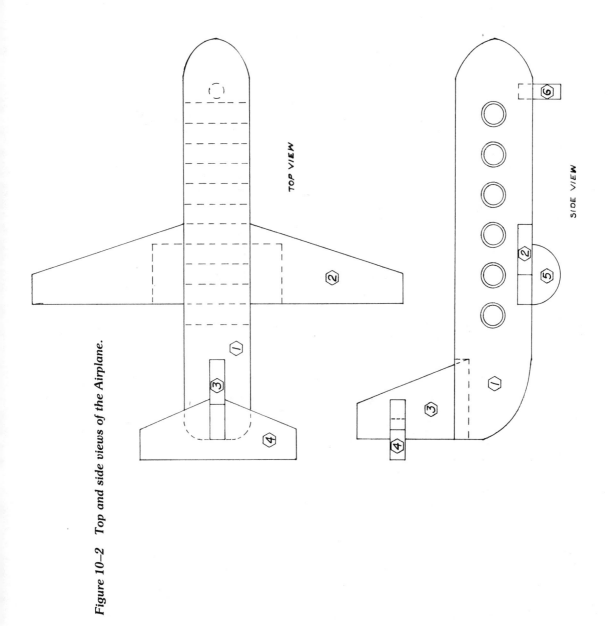

TOP VIEW

SIDE VIEW

Figure 10-2 Top and side views of the Airplane.

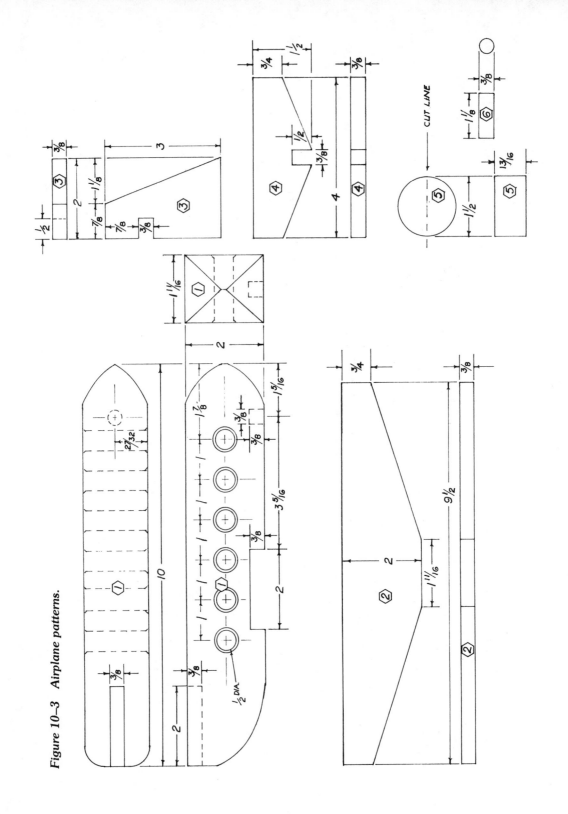

Figure 10–3 Airplane patterns.

·11·
Fire Truck

Figure 11–1

The Fire Truck has nearly everything a child needs to race to the scene of the action. All he has to do is provide the siren.

PART	DIMENSIONS (thickness x width x length)	QUANTITY
1. Side	$\frac{1}{2}$ x 3 x $7\frac{7}{16}$	2
2. Fender	$\frac{13}{16}$ x $2\frac{1}{2}$ x 15	2
3. Wheel	$\frac{13}{16}$ x $2\frac{1}{2}$ dia.	4
4. Base	$\frac{13}{16}$ x $3\frac{1}{4}$ x 15	1
5. Fire Wall	$\frac{1}{2}$ x $2\frac{1}{2}$ x $3\frac{1}{4}$	1
6. Engine	$2\frac{3}{4}$ x 2 x $2\frac{1}{2}$	1
7. Radiator	$\frac{1}{2}$ x $2\frac{1}{4}$ x $3\frac{1}{4}$	1
8. Steering Post	$\frac{3}{8}$ dia. x $3\frac{1}{2}$	1
9. Head Lamp	$\frac{3}{4}$ dia. x 1	2
10. Steering Wheel	$\frac{13}{16}$ x $1\frac{1}{8}$ dia.	1
11. Ladder Hanger	$\frac{1}{2}$ x $1\frac{13}{16}$ x $2\frac{1}{2}$	4
12. Ladder Rail	$\frac{1}{2}$ x $\frac{1}{2}$ x 7	4
13. Bumper	$\frac{1}{2}$ x $1\frac{1}{16}$ x $4\frac{7}{8}$	1
14. Ladder Rung	$\frac{1}{4}$ dia. x $1\frac{1}{2}$	14
15. Axle	$\frac{3}{8}$ dia. x $4\frac{1}{4}$	2
16. Water Pump	$1\frac{13}{16}$ dia. x $2\frac{1}{8}$	1
17. Pump Motor	1 x $1\frac{1}{4}$ x $1\frac{7}{8}$	1
18. Bed	$\frac{13}{16}$ x $2\frac{1}{4}$ x 6	1
19. Bed Brace	$\frac{13}{16}$ x $\frac{15}{16}$ x $2\frac{1}{4}$	2
20. Seat Back	$\frac{13}{16}$ x $1\frac{1}{4}$ x $2\frac{1}{4}$	1

Construction

1. Redraw the Fire Truck patterns to full scale, using the dimensions shown in Figures 11–4, 11–5, and 11–6.
2. Select the amount of clean, blemish-free hardwood stock needed to complete the Fire Truck.
3. If not already milled, mill the rough 1″ woodstock to $\frac{13}{16}$″ thickness.
4. Laminate enough 1″ woodstock together to achieve the desired thickness for the engine ⑥, water pump ⑯, and pump motor ⑰. Glue and clamp the wood together and allow to dry.
5. Prepare the production patterns as needed. Label each pattern for later use.
6. Place the milled woodstock on a worktable and draw or trace all of the Fire Truck parts onto it.
7. For ease of handling, cut the hardwood to rough lengths on the radial arm saw. Do not cut through any toy parts during this process.
8. Joint the edges of the milled woodstock on the jointer. This provides a straight edge to guide future cuts on the table saw and radial arm saw.
9. On the table saw or radial arm saw, cut the following parts to the exact rectangular dimensions listed previously.

1	Sides	12	Ladder Rails
2	Fenders	13	Bumper
4	Base	17	Pump Motor
5	Fire Wall	18	Bed
6	Engine	19	Bed Brace
7	Radiator	23	Seat Back
11	Ladder Hangers		

10. Re-saw the following parts to the desired thickness on the table saw. See drawings for details.

1	Sides	11	Ladder Hangers
5	Fire Wall	12	Ladder Rails
7	Radiator	13	Bumper

11. Cut the following parts to shape on the band saw, allowing a small amount of wood to remain outside the pencil lines so that final shaping and sanding can be done on the disc or belt sander.

1	Sides (cut steps of the sides only)	8	Steering Post
2	Fenders	9	Head Lamps
3	Wheels	10	Steering Wheel
6	Engine (cut the curved part only)	11	Ladder Hangers
		14	Ladder Rungs
		15	Axles

12. Disc or belt sand the following parts to exact size and shape.

1	Sides (belt sand the steps with 1″ belt sander)	9	Head Lamps (taper ends slightly)
2	Fenders	10	Steering Wheel
3	Wheels	11	Ladder Hangers
6	Engine	14	Ladder Rungs (taper ends slightly)
8	Steering Post (taper ends slightly)	15	Axles (taper ends slightly)

13. Drill ⅜″ holes into the following parts. See drawings for details.

3	Wheel (axle hole)
4	Base (axle housing holes, steering post hole)
10	Steering Wheel

14. Drill ¼″ holes into the ladder rails 12. See drawings for details.

15. Remove all of the sharp edges and corners with a router or sandpaper.

16. Belt sand all of the flat surfaces of the fire truck, sanding with the grain to prevent scratches.

17. Shape the water pump on the wood lathe or disc or belt sander.

Assembly

1. Glue and dowel the fenders 2 to the base 4.
2. Glue the bed 10, bed braces 19, sides 1, and seat back 20, to the base 4.

Note: You may find it more convenient to glue individual sections together first, after which they can then be glued and doweled to the base 4 much easier.

3. Glue and dowel the remaining parts and sections to the base 4. Follow the procedure described in the Introduction.
4. Insert the axles 15 into the axle holes of the base 4 and then glue the wheels 3 to the axles 15.
5. Sand the surface of the Fire Truck to remove scratches and blemishes.
6. Apply one or two coats of boiled linseed oil to the surface.

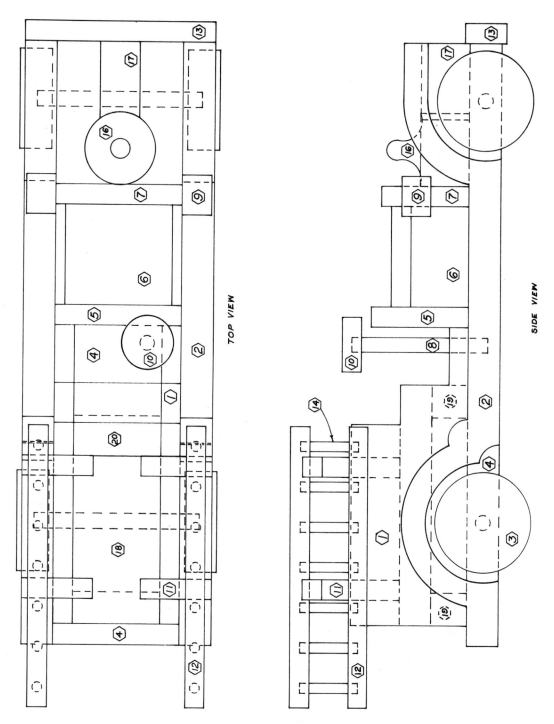

TOP VIEW

SIDE VIEW

Figure 11–2 Top and side views of Fire Truck.

63

FRONT VIEW

Figure 11–3 Front view of Fire Truck.

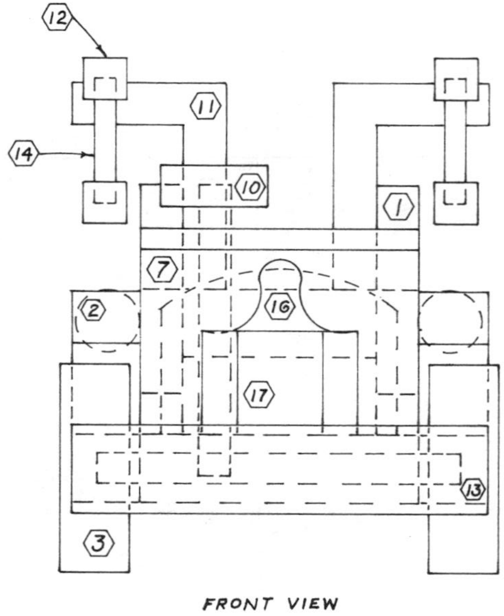

64

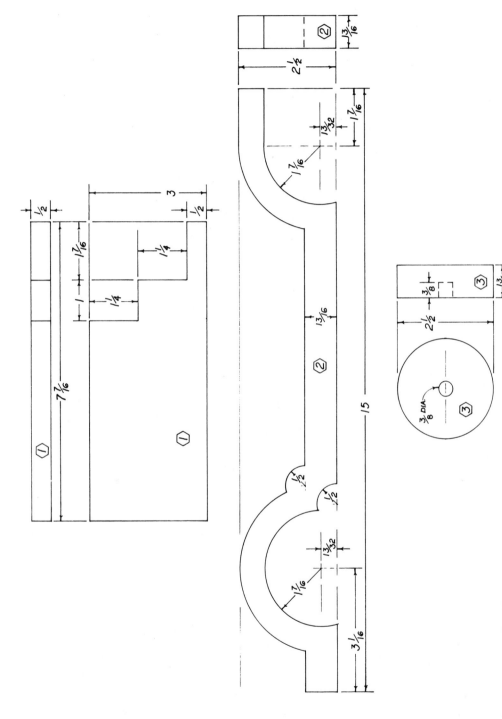

Figure 11-4 Fire Truck patterns.

Figure 11–5 Fire Truck patterns.

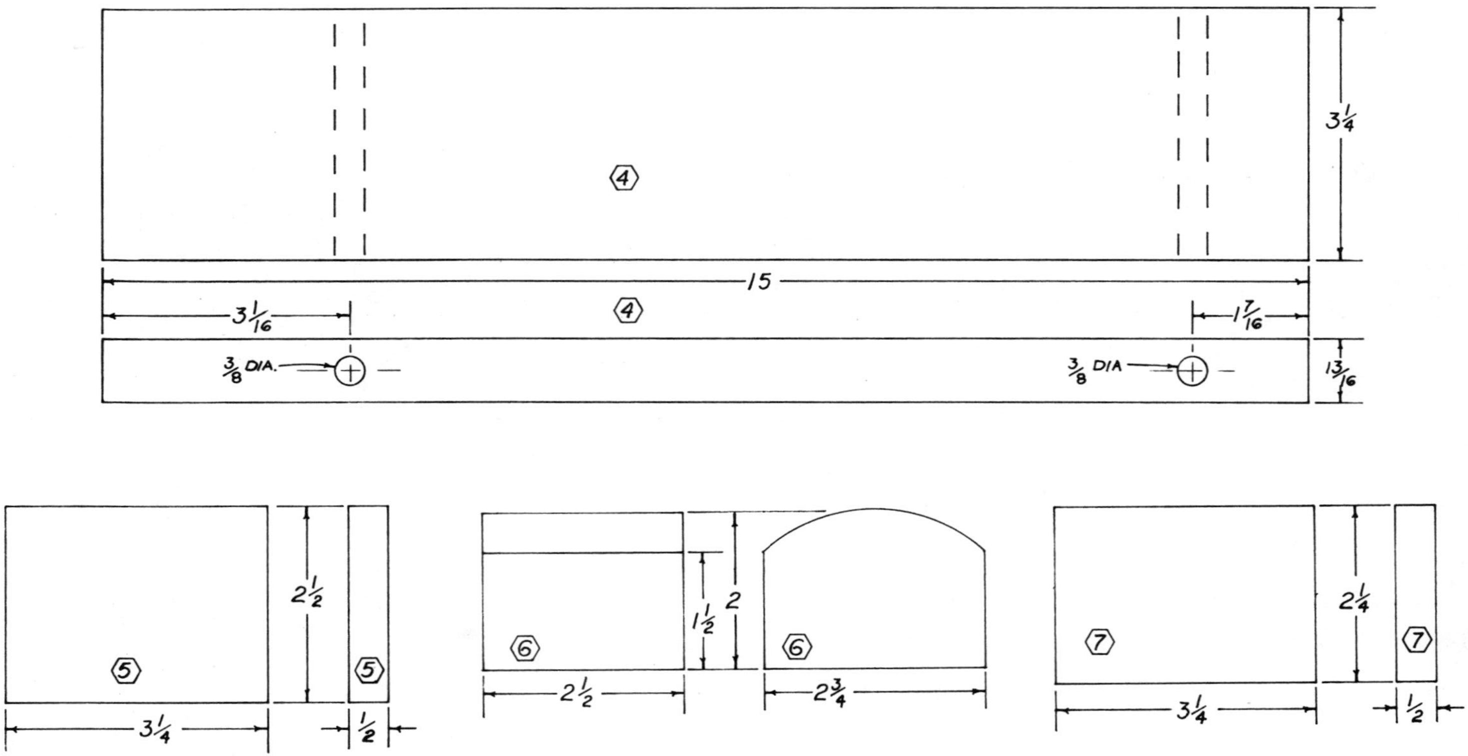

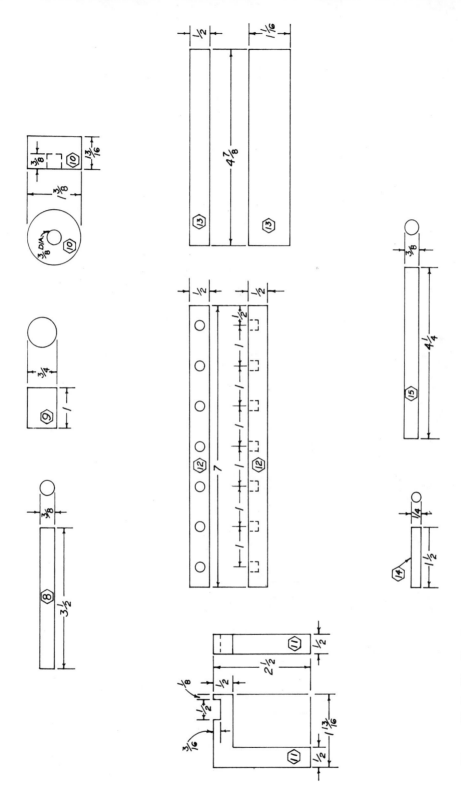

Figure 11-6 Fire Truck patterns.

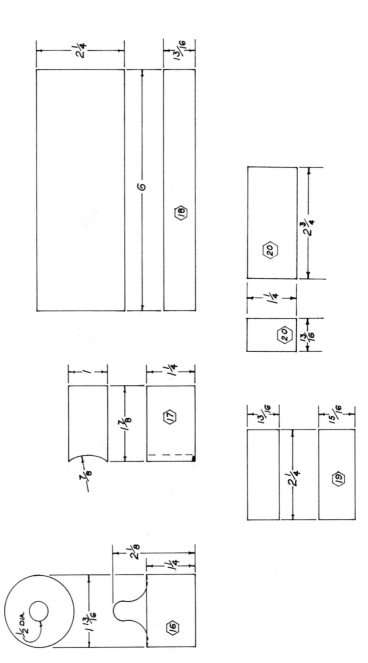

Figure 11–7 Fire Truck patterns.

·12·
Super Model T

Figure 12–1

Early transportation was not only an adventure but a challenge
to the automobile operator as well. The child can now
experience this adventure with the Super Model T.

PART	DIMENSIONS (thickness x width x length)	QUANTITY
1. Cab Roof	$\frac{13}{16}$ x 4 x 5	1
2. Cab Back Side	$\frac{13}{16}$ x 4 x $7\frac{1}{4}$	1
3. Cab Post	$\frac{3}{8}$ dia. x $4\frac{3}{4}$	2
4. Cab Seat Back	$\frac{13}{16}$ x $2\frac{3}{8}$ x $3\frac{1}{8}$	1
5. Cab Seat	$1\frac{7}{8}$ x 2 x $2\frac{3}{8}$	1
6. Dash	$\frac{1}{2}$ x 1 x $2\frac{3}{8}$	1
7. Trunk	2 x 3 x 4	1
8. Cab Side	$\frac{13}{16}$ x 3 x $3\frac{3}{32}$	2
9. Fender	$\frac{13}{16}$ x $2\frac{13}{16}$ x 12	2
10. Base	$\frac{13}{16}$ x 4 x 11	1
11. Axle Housing Brace	$\frac{13}{16}$ x $1\frac{1}{2}$ x $2\frac{1}{2}$	2
12. Wheel	$\frac{13}{16}$ x $3\frac{1}{2}$ dia.	4
13. Axle Housing	$\frac{13}{16}$ x $2\frac{1}{2}$ x 4	2
14. Axle	$\frac{3}{8}$ dia. x 5	2
15. Engine	$2\frac{3}{4}$ x $2\frac{1}{2}$ x 3	1
16. Radiator	$\frac{13}{16}$ x $2\frac{1}{2}$ x 3	1
17. Radiator Cap	$\frac{1}{4}$ dia. x $\frac{5}{8}$	1
18. Fire Wall	$\frac{13}{16}$ x $3\frac{1}{2}$ x 4	1
19. Head Lamp	$\frac{3}{4}$ dia. x 1	2

Construction

1. Redraw the Super Model T pattern pieces to full scale, using the dimensions shown in Figures 12–6, 12–7, and 12–8.
2. Select the amount of clean, blemish-free hardwood stock needed to complete the Super Model T.
3. Mill the 1″ hardwood stock to $\frac{13}{16}$″ thickness.
4. Laminate enough $\frac{13}{16}$″ stock together to achieve the desired thickness for the cab seat 5, trunk 7, and engine 15. Glue and clamp the wood together and allow to dry.
5. Prepare the production patterns as needed. Label each pattern for later use.
6. Place the milled woodstock on a worktable and draw or trace the parts of the Super "T" Model on to the milled hardwood.
7. For easier handling, cut the hardwood parts to rough lengths approximately 8″ long on the radial arm saw. Be careful not to cut through a toy part during this process.
8. Joint the edges of the milled woodstock on the jointer to provide a straight edge to guide future cuts.
9. On the table saw or radial arm saw, cut the following parts to the exact rectangular dimensions listed previously.

1 Cab Roof	9 Fenders
2 Cab Back Side	10 Base
4 Cab Seat Back	11 Axle Housing Braces
5 Cab Seat	13 Axle Housings
6 Dash	15 Engine
7 Trunk	16 Radiator
8 Cab Sides	19 Fire Wall

10. Drill ⅜″ holes into the following parts. See drawings for details.

| 1 Cab Roof | 12 Wheels |
| 8 Cab Sides | 13 Axle Housings |

11. Drill a ¼″ hole into the radiator 16 for the radiator cap 17.

12. Cut the angles on the following parts on the table saw, or radial arm saw.

1 Cab Roof	8 Cab Sides
2 Cab Back Side	10 Base (front)
4 Cab Seat Back	11 Axle Housing Brace
5 Cab Seat	13 Axle Housings
6 Dash	

Some of the angles can be cut out on the band saw. Do not cut into the pencil lines if the band saw is used. The parts will be finished on the disc sander.

13. Cut the following parts on the band saw.

3 Cab Posts	14 Axles
7 Trunk	17 Radiator Cap
9 Fenders	19 Head Lamps
12 Wheels	

Do not cut into the pencil lines. Allow a small amount of wood to remain outside the pencil lines so that the final finishing can be done on the disc or belt sander.

14. Disc or belt sand the following parts to exact size and shape.

3 Cab Posts	12 Wheels
7 Trunk	14 Axles
9 Fenders (sand on a 1″ belt sander)	17 Radiator Cap
	19 Head Lamps

Slightly taper the ends of the cab posts, axles, radiator cap, and one side of the head lamps. Then flatten one side of the cab posts, axles, and radiator cap about ½″ up from each end. This will allow excess glue to escape and prevent the wood from splitting when the parts are tapped into the dowel holes.

15. Remove all of the sharp edges and corners with a router or sandpaper.

16. Belt sand all of the flat surfaces to remove scratches and blemishes. Always sand with the woodgrain, not across it, to prevent scratches.

Assembly

Note: For how to glue and dowel parts together, see the procedure described in the Introduction.

1. Glue the following parts together to form the cab.

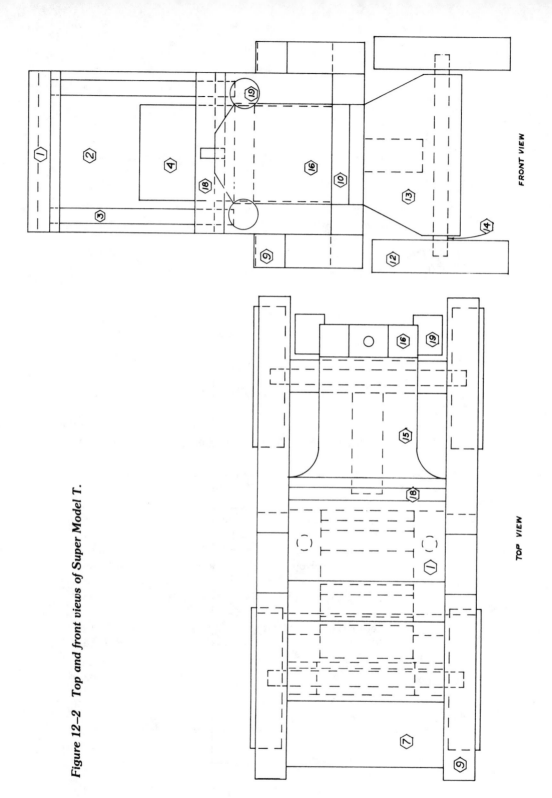

FRONT VIEW

TOP VIEW

Figure 12-2   Top and front views of Super Model T.

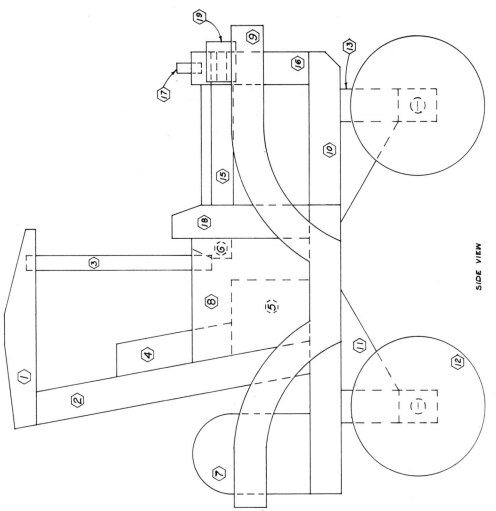

SIDE VIEW

Figure 12–3   Side view of Super Model T.

|1| Cab Roof
|2| Cab Back Side
|3| Cab Posts

|8| Cab Sides
|19| Fire Wall

2. Glue and dowel the axle housing |13| and axle housing braces |11| to the base |10|.

3. Glue and dowel the fenders |9| to the base |10|. Position the fenders as shown in the drawings. Gluing and doweling the fenders so they are out of slightly alignment with the rest of the car body can enhance the "old-time" appeal of the "Super "T" Model.

4. Glue and dowel the completed cab section, trunk |7|, engine |15|, and radiator |16| to the base |10|.

5. Insert the axles |14| into the axle holes of the axle housing |13| and then glue the wheels |12| to the axles |14|.

6. Glue the remaining parts to the body of the Super Model T. See drawings for details.

|4| Cab Seat Back
|5| Cab Seat
|6| Dash

|16| Radiator
|17| Radiator Cap
|19| Head Lamps

7. Sand all of the surfaces of the Super Model T smooth with medium or fine grit sandpaper.

8. Apply one or two coats of boiled linseed oil to finish the surface.

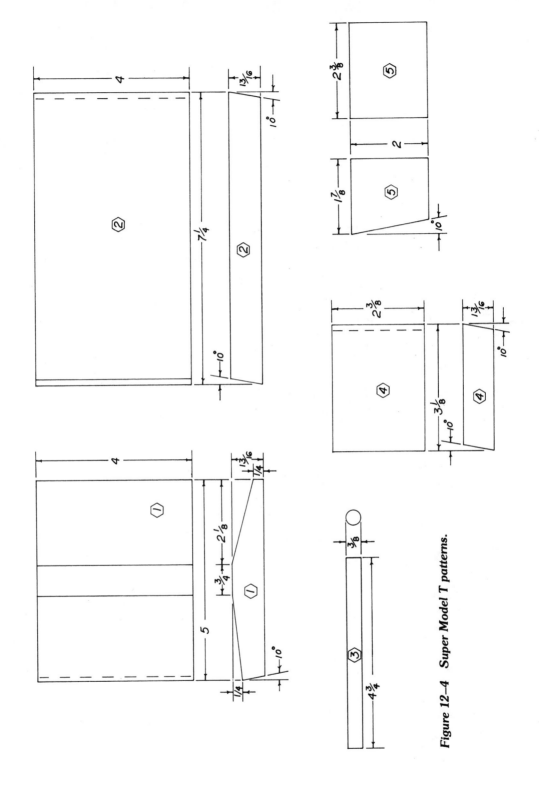

Figure 12-4 Super Model T patterns.

75

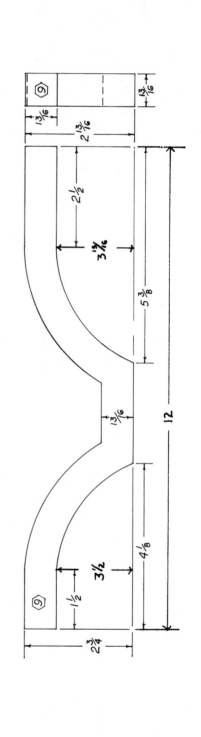

Figure 12–5 Super Model T patterns.

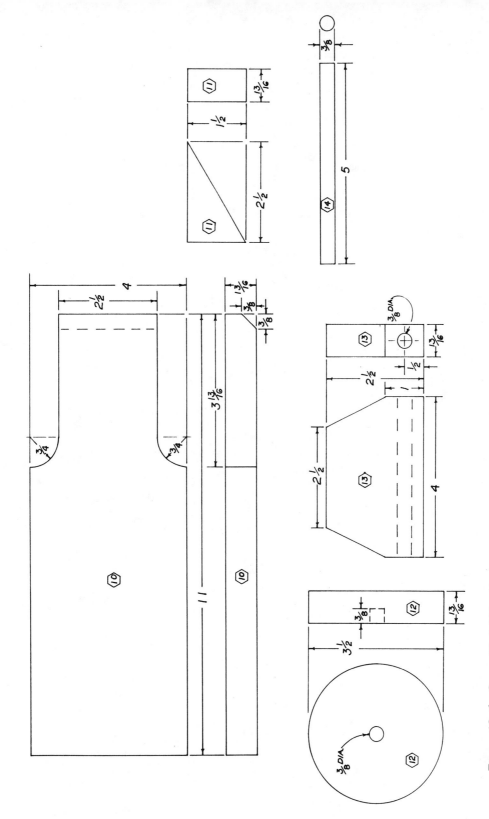

Figure 12–6 Super Model T patterns.

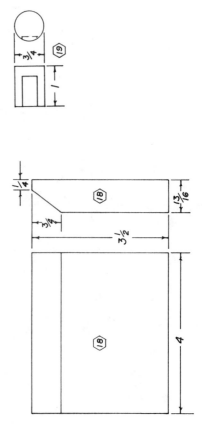

Figure 12–7 Super Model T patterns.

·13·
The Runabout

Figure 13–1

The horseless carriage was one of the wonders of yesteryear.
It is easy to recreate it in wood today.

PART	DIMENSIONS (thickness x width x length)	QUANTITY
1. Cab Roof	$\frac{13}{16}$ x 4 x $4\frac{3}{4}$	1
2. Cab Back	$\frac{1}{2}$ x 4 x 5	1
3. Seat Back	$\frac{1}{2}$ x $2\frac{3}{4}$ x 4	2
4. Cab Post	$\frac{3}{8}$ dia. x $4\frac{7}{8}$	2
5. Seat	$\frac{13}{16}$ x $1\frac{1}{2}$ x 4	2
6. Sides	$\frac{13}{16}$ x 2 x $7\frac{3}{16}$	2
7. Grill	$\frac{13}{16}$ x $2\frac{1}{2}$ x 4	1
8. Base	$\frac{13}{16}$ x 4 x $9\frac{1}{4}$	1
9. Rear Axle Housing	$\frac{13}{16}$ x $1\frac{1}{4}$ x $3\frac{1}{8}$	2
10. Front Axle Housing	$\frac{13}{16}$ x $1\frac{1}{4}$ x $4\frac{5}{8}$	2
11. Wheel	$\frac{13}{16}$ x $3\frac{1}{2}$ dia.	4
12. Axle	$\frac{3}{8}$ dia. x 5	2

Construction

1. Redraw The Runabout pattern pieces to full scale, using the dimensions shown in Figures 13–4 and 13–5.
2. Select the amount of clean, blemish-free hardwood stock needed to complete The Runabout.
3. If not already milled, mill the 1″ hardwood stock to $\frac{13}{16}$″ thickness.
4. Prepare the production patterns as needed. Label each pattern for later use.
5. Place the milled woodstock on a worktable and draw or trace the toy parts onto it.
6. For easier handling, cut the hardwood parts to rough lengths approximately 8″ long on the radial arm saw. Be careful not to cut through any toy parts during this process.
7. Joint the edges of the milled woodstock on the jointer. This gives a straight edge to guide future cuts on the table or radial arm saw.
8. On the table saw or radial arm saw, cut the following parts to the exact rectangular dimensions listed previously.
   - [1] Cab Roof
   - [2] Cab Back
   - [3] Seat Backs
   - [5] Seats
   - [6] Sides
   - [7] Grill
   - [8] Base
   - [9] Rear Axle Housing
   - [10] Front Axle Housing
9. Re-saw the following parts to $\frac{1}{2}$″ thickness on the table saw.
   - [2] Cab Back
   - [3] Seat Backs
10. Cut the following parts out on the band saw.

6	Sides (front curves)	10	Front Axle Housing
7	Grill	11	Wheels
9	Rear Axle Housing		

When cutting parts on the band saw, do not cut into the pencil lines. Allow a small amount of excess wood to extend beyond the pencil lines so that the final finish and shaping can be done on the disc or belt sanders.

11. Disc sand the following parts to size and shape.

| 7 | Grill | 10 | Front Axle Housing |
| 9 | Rear Axle Housing | 11 | Wheels |

12. Drill ⅜" holes into the following parts. See drawings for details.

1	Cab Roof	10	Front Axle Housing
5	Seats	11	Wheels
9	Rear Axle Housing		

13. Remove all sharp edges and corners with the router or sandpaper.
14. Belt sand all of the flat surfaces to a smooth finish, sanding with the grain to prevent scratches.

Assembly

Note: For how to glue and dowel parts together, see the procedure described in the Introduction.

1. Glue and dowel the axle housings 9 and 10 to the base 8.
2. Glue and dowel the grill 7 to the base 8.
3. Glue and dowel the sides 6 to the base 8.
4. Glue and dowel the seats 5, seat backs 3, cab back 2 to the sides 6.
5. Glue the cab posts 4 to the cab roof 1 and front seat 5. Glue and dowel the cab roof 1 to the cab back 2.
6. Place the axles 12 into the axle holes of the axle housings 9 and 10 and then glue the wheels 11 to the axles 12.
7. Sand the surface with medium or fine grit sandpaper.
8. Apply one or two coats of boiled linseed oil.

Figure 13–2 Top and front views of The Runabout.

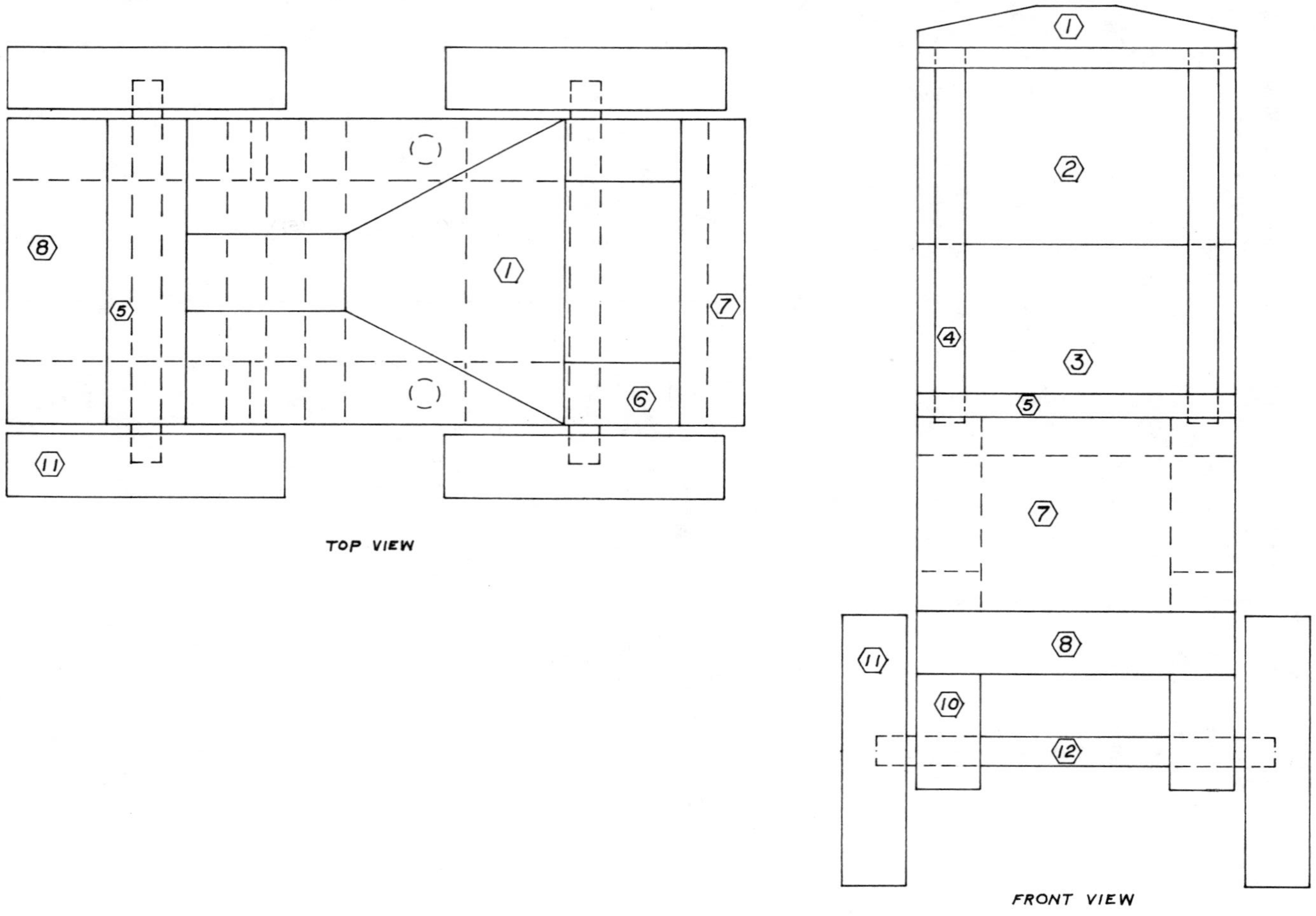

FRONT VIEW

TOP VIEW

82

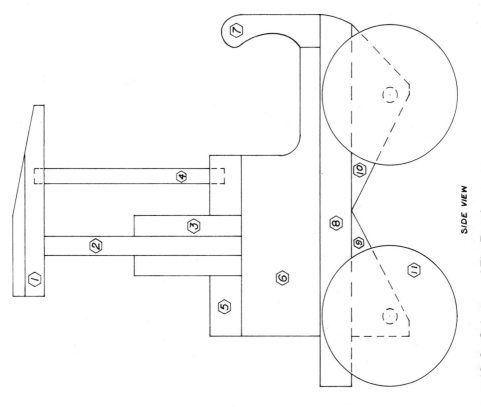

SIDE VIEW

Figure 13–3   Side view of The Runabout.

83

Figure 13-4   The Runabout patterns.

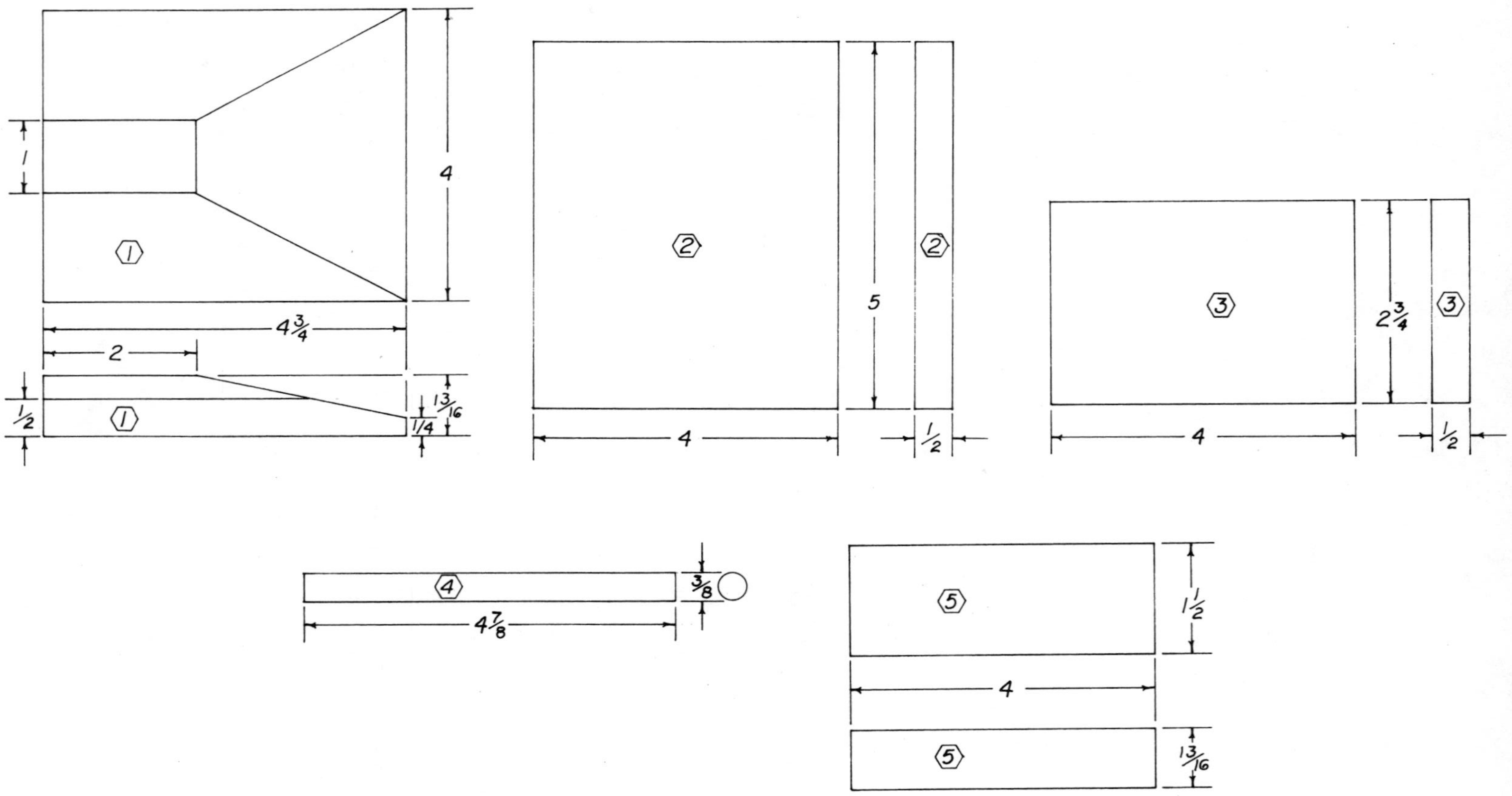

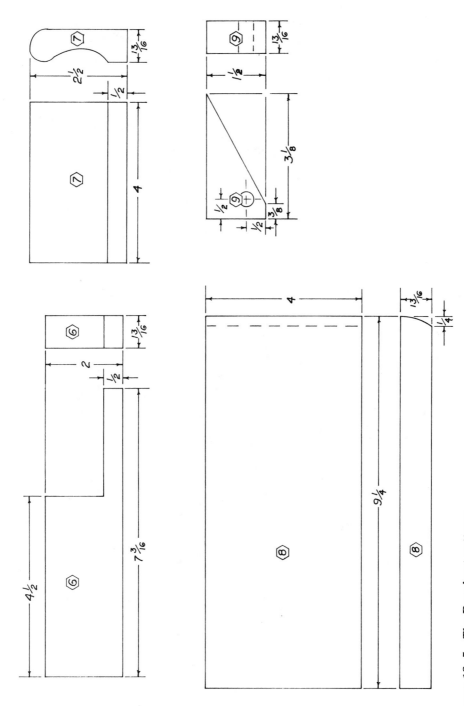

Figure 13–5   The Runabout patterns.

85

Figure 13–6   The Runabout patterns.

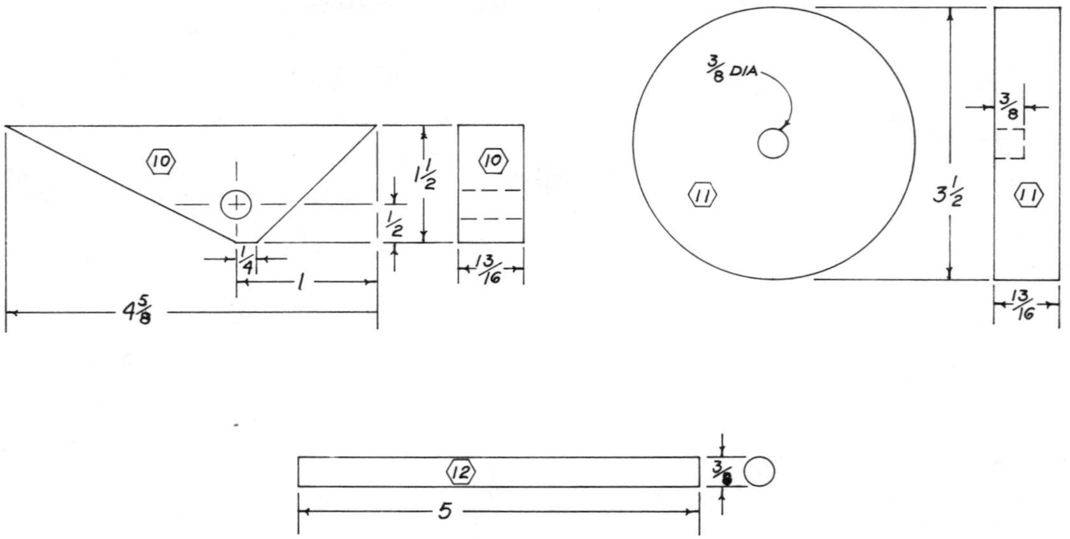

·14·
Race Car

Figure 14–1

The Race Car is for fast getaways and quick turns—an absolute necessity for the playroom traveler.

PART	DIMENSIONS (thickness x width x length)	QUANTITY
1. Wheel	$\frac{13}{16}$ x 2 dia.	4
2. Fender	$\frac{13}{16}$ x $1\frac{5}{8}$ x 8	2
3. Front Hood	$\frac{3}{4}$ x $2\frac{3}{8}$ x 3	1
4. Engine	$\frac{13}{16}$ x $2\frac{3}{8}$ x $2\frac{1}{2}$	1
5. Base	$\frac{13}{16}$ x $2\frac{3}{8}$ x 8	1
6. Axle	$\frac{3}{8}$ dia. x $5\frac{1}{8}$	2
7. Exhaust Pipe	$\frac{1}{4}$ dia. (cut to length)	6
8. Seat Back	$\frac{3}{8}$ x $1\frac{3}{8}$ x $2\frac{3}{8}$	1

Construction

1. Redraw the Race Car pattern pieces to full scale, using the dimensions shown in Figure 14–4.
2. Select the amount of clean, blemish-free hardwood stock needed to complete the project.
3. If not already milled, mill the rough 1″ woodstock to $\frac{13}{16}$″ thickness.
4. Prepare the production patterns as needed and label each for later use.
5. Place the milled woodstock on a worktable and draw or trace all of the Race Car parts onto it.
6. For easier handling, cut the hardwood parts to rough lengths approximately 8″ long on the radial arm saw. Be careful not to cut through any toy parts during this process.
7. Joint the edges of the milled woodstock on the jointer. This provides a flat edge to guide future cuts on the table saw and radial arm saw.
8. On the table saw or radial arm saw, cut the following parts to the exact rectangular dimensions listed previously.
    - 2 Fenders
    - 3 Front Hood
    - 4 Engine
    - 5 Base
    - 8 Seat Back
9. Re-saw the seat back 8 to $\frac{1}{2}$″ thickness on the table saw.
10. Cut the taper of the fenders 2 on the band saw and then smooth the edges on the disc sander. This can also be done on the table saw if you build a taper jig.
11. Cut the engine 4 angle on the table saw. See drawings for details.
12. Cut the following parts out on the band saw, being careful not to cut into the pencil lines.
    - 1 Wheels
    - 6 Axles
    - 7 Exhaust Pipes (cut to length)
13. Disc sand the following parts to size and shape. Taper the ends of the axles slightly and shape the exhaust pipes as desired.

      1 Wheels
      6 Axles
      7 Exhaust Pipes
14. Drill $\frac{3}{8}''$ holes into the following parts.
      1 Wheels
      2 Fenders
      5 Base
15. Drill $\frac{1}{4}''$ holes into the engine 4 block for the exhaust pipes 7 .
16. Remove all of the sharp edges and corners with the router and rounding bit or with sandpaper.
17. Belt sand all of the flat surfaces, sanding with the grain to prevent scratches.

Assembly

Note: For how to glue and dowel parts together, see the procedure described in the Introduction.

1. Glue and dowel the fenders 2 to the base 5 . Be sure to align the axle holes of the fenders 2 with the axle holes of the base 5 . If they are not properly aligned, it may be necessary to re-drill the axle holes after the butt joints have dried.
2. Glue the hood 3 , engine 4 , and the seat back 8 to the base 5 .
3. Glue the exhaust pipes 7 to the engine 4 .
4. Place the axles 6 into the axle holes of the base 5 and then glue the wheels 1 to the axles 6 .
5. Sand all the surfaces of the race car with medium or fine grit sandpaper.
6. Apply one or two coats of linseed oil to the surface.

Figure 14–2   Top, side, and front views of the Race Car.

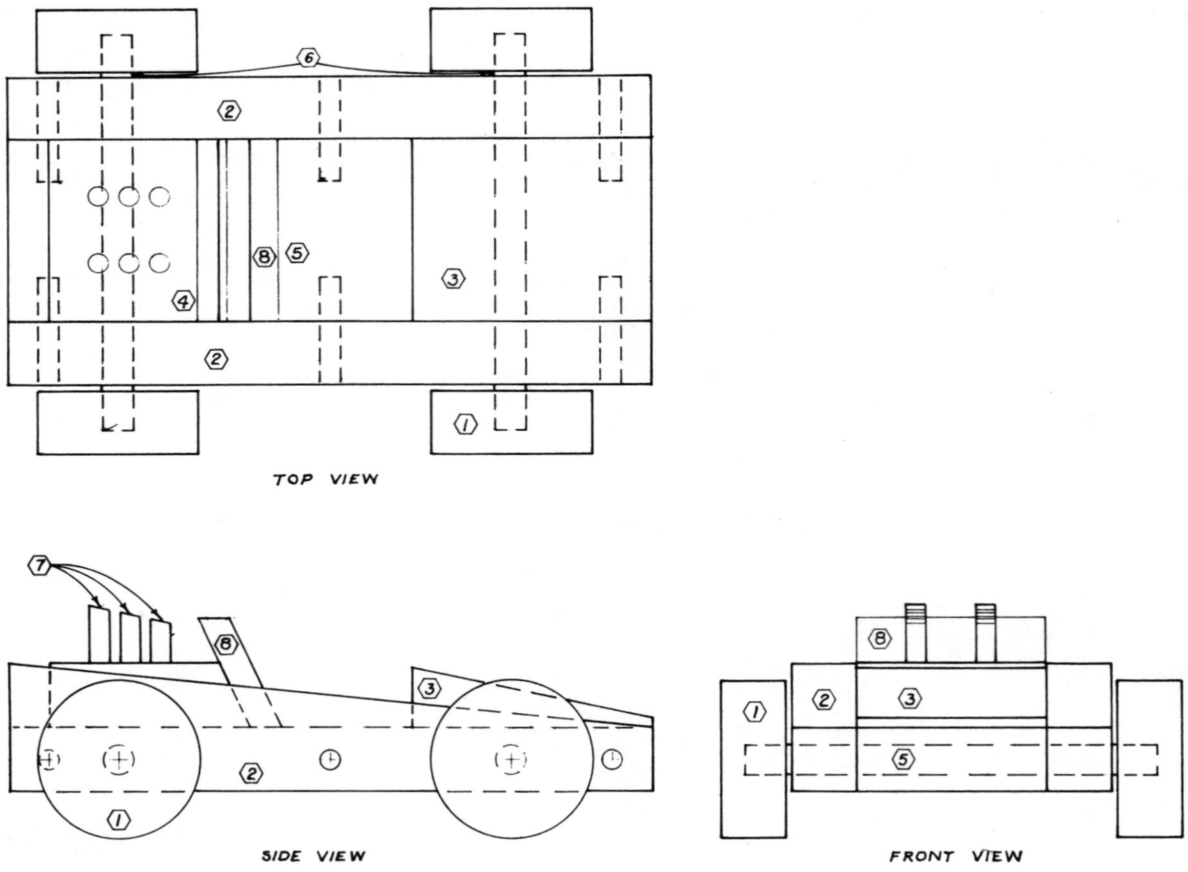

TOP VIEW

SIDE VIEW

FRONT VIEW

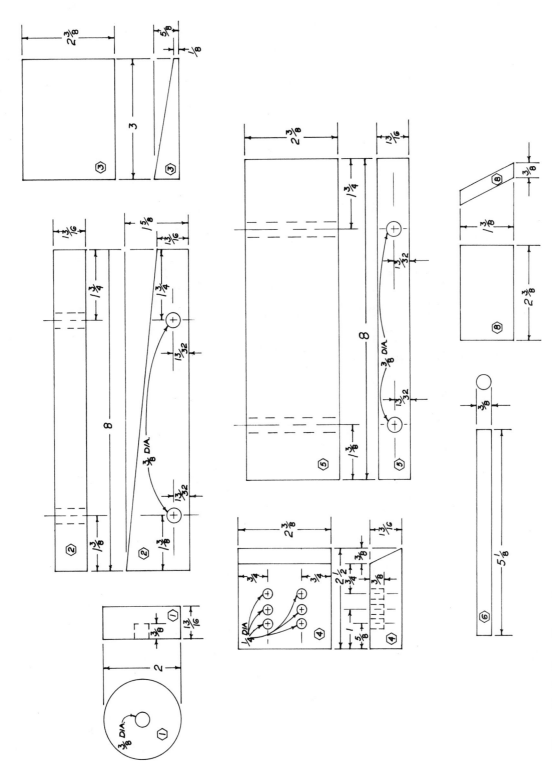

Figure 14–3   Race Car patterns.

91

·15·
Trailer Truck Cab

Figure 15–1
Truck Cab, shown with trailer (see Chapter 16).

The Trailer Truck is handy for moving loads of blocks or other toys from place to place. Project 15 is for the cab. Project 16 has instructions for building the trailer.

PART	DIMENSIONS (thickness x width x length)	QUANTITY
1. Roof	$\frac{13}{16}$ x $4\frac{1}{8}$ x $5\frac{1}{16}$	1
2. Side	$\frac{13}{16}$ x $4\frac{1}{4}$ x $4\frac{1}{2}$	2 (R & L)
3. Grill	$\frac{13}{16}$ x $4\frac{1}{2}$ x $4\frac{1}{2}$	1
4. Base	$\frac{13}{16}$ x $2\frac{7}{8}$ x $7\frac{5}{16}$	1
5. Wheel	$1\frac{5}{8}$ x $2\frac{1}{4}$ dia.	4
6. Hitch	1 x $\frac{7}{8}$ x $2\frac{1}{2}$	1
7. Bumper	$\frac{1}{2}$ x $\frac{13}{16}$ x $4\frac{1}{2}$	1
8. Axle	$\frac{3}{8}$ dia. x $3\frac{7}{8}$	2

Construction

1. Redraw the truck cab patterns to full scale, using the dimensions shown in Figures 15–3 and 15–4.
2. Select the amount of clean, blemish-free hardwood stock needed to complete the truck.
3. If not already milled, mill the rough 1″ woodstock to $\frac{13}{16}$″ thickness.
4. Laminate enough $\frac{13}{16}$″ stock together to achieve the desired thickness for the wheels ⑤ and hitch ⑥. Glue and clamp the wood together and allow to dry.
5. Prepare the production patterns as needed, and label each for later use.
6. Place the milled woodstock on a worktable and draw or trace all of the truck parts onto it.
7. For easier handling, cut the hardwood into pieces approximately 8″ long or longer on the radial arm saw, being careful not to cut through any toy parts.
8. Joint the edges of the milled woodstock on the jointer. This provides a straight edge to guide future cuts on the table saw and radial arm saw.
9. On the table saw or radial arm saw, cut the following parts to the exact rectangular dimensions listed previously.
   ① Roof   ④ Base
   ② Sides (R & L)   ⑥ Hitch
   ③ Grill   ⑦ Bumper
10. Cut the angular slopes of the following parts on the table saw. See drawings for details.
    ① Roof   ③ Grill
    ② Sides (R & L)   ⑥ Hitch
11. Cut the following parts out on the band saw.
    ⑤ Wheels
    ⑧ Axles
    Do not cut into the pencil lines. Final shaping will be done on the disc sander.
12. Cut the windows and fender wells out with a circle saw on the drill press. See drawings for details.
13. Drill suitable sized holes into the following parts. See drawings for details.

    4 Base (axle hole)

    5 Wheel (axle hole)

    6 Hitch (hitch hole)

14. Disc sand the wheels 5 to shape and slightly taper the ends of the axles 8 .

15. Remove all of the sharp edges and corners with the router or sandpaper.

Assembly

Note: For how to glue and dowel parts together, see the procedure described in the Introduction.

1. Glue and dowel the following parts together.

    1 Roof   4 Base

    2 Sides   6 Hitch

    3 Front   7 Bumper

2. Belt sand all of the flat surfaces of the truck after the butt joints have dried. Sand with the grain of the wood to prevent scratches.

3. Place the axles 8 into the axle holes of the base 4 and then glue the wheels 5 to the axles 8 .

4. Apply one or two coats of boiled linseed oil to the surface of the truck.

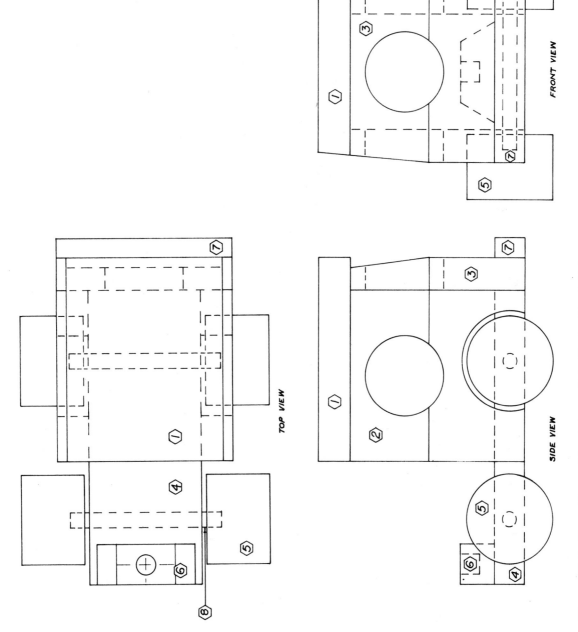

TOP VIEW

FRONT VIEW

SIDE VIEW

Figure 15–2 Top, side, and front views of the Trailer Truck Cab.

95

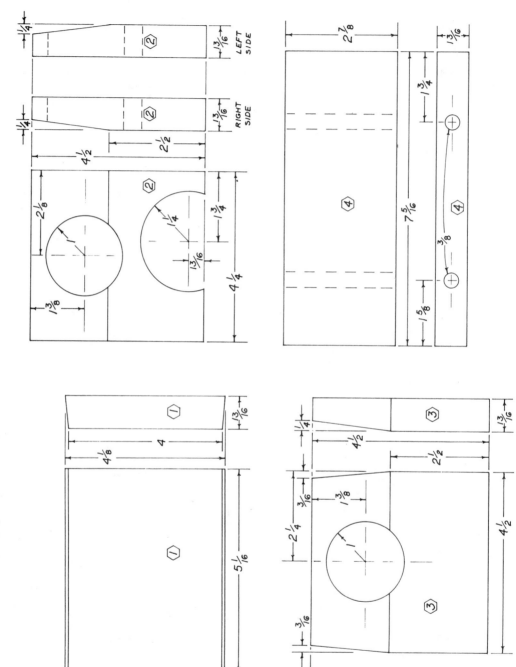

Figure 15–3   Trailer Truck Cab patterns.

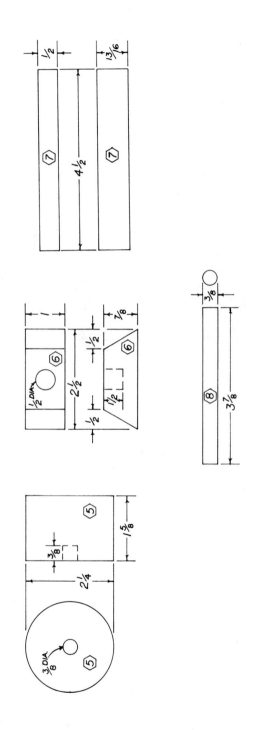

Figure 15–4 Trailer Truck Cab patterns.

·16·
Truck Trailer

Figure 16–1
Truck Trailer, shown with Cab (see Chapter 15).

The Truck Trailer goes with the cab built in Project 15.

PART	DIMENSIONS	QUANTITY
	(thickness x width x length)	
1. Wheel	$\frac{13}{16}$ x $2\frac{1}{4}$ dia.	2
2. Bed	$\frac{13}{16}$ x $3\frac{3}{4}$ x 12	1
3. Hitch	$\frac{1}{2}$ dia. x $1\frac{9}{16}$	1
4. Rear Axle Housing	$\frac{13}{16}$ x $1\frac{5}{8}$ x $3\frac{3}{4}$	1
5. Rear Axle	$\frac{3}{8}$ dia. x $4\frac{3}{4}$	1

Construction

1. Redraw the Truck Trailer patterns to full scale, using the dimensions shown in Figure 16–3.
2. Select the amount of clean, blemish-free hardwood stock needed to complete the Truck Trailer.
3. If not already milled, mill the rough 1″ woodstock to $\frac{13}{16}$″ thickness.
4. Prepare the production patterns as needed. Label them for future use.
5. Place the milled woodstock on a worktable and draw or trace all of the trailer parts onto it.
6. For easier handling, cut the hardwood into rough lengths approximately 8″ long on the radial arm saw. Be sure not to cut through any toy parts.
7. Joint the edges of the milled woodstock on the jointer. This provides a straight edge to guide future cuts on the table saw and radial arm saw.
8. Cut the following parts to their exact rectangular dimensions on the table saw or radial arm saw.
   - [2] Bed
   - [5] Rear Axle Housing

   Cut the grooves into the bed [2].
9. Cut the following parts out on the band saw.
   - [1] Wheels
   - [5] Rear Axle

   Do not cut into the pencil lines—allow for finish work on the disc sander.
10. Disc sand the following parts to shape.
    - [1] Wheels
    - [5] Rear Axle (taper ends slightly)
11. Drill suitably sized holes into the following parts. See drawings for details.
    - [1] Wheels (axle holes)
    - [2] Bed (hitch hole)
    - [5] Rear Axle Housing (axle hole)
12. Belt sand all of the flat surfaces to a smooth finish. Always sand with the grain to avoid scratching the surface.
13. Remove all sharp edges and corners with router or sandpaper.

Assembly

1. Glue and dowel all of the parts together, following the procedure described in the Introduction. The parts may be joined in any sequence that seems convenient.
2. Apply one or two coats of boiled linseed oil to the surface.

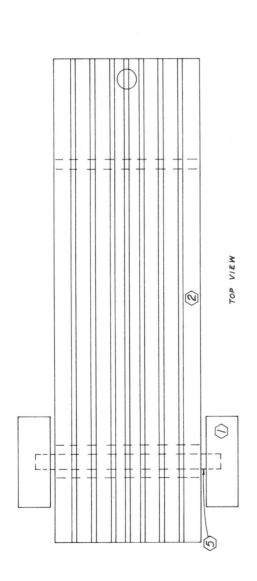

Figure 16–2 Top, side, and front views of the Truck Trailer.

Figure 16–3 Truck Trailer patterns.

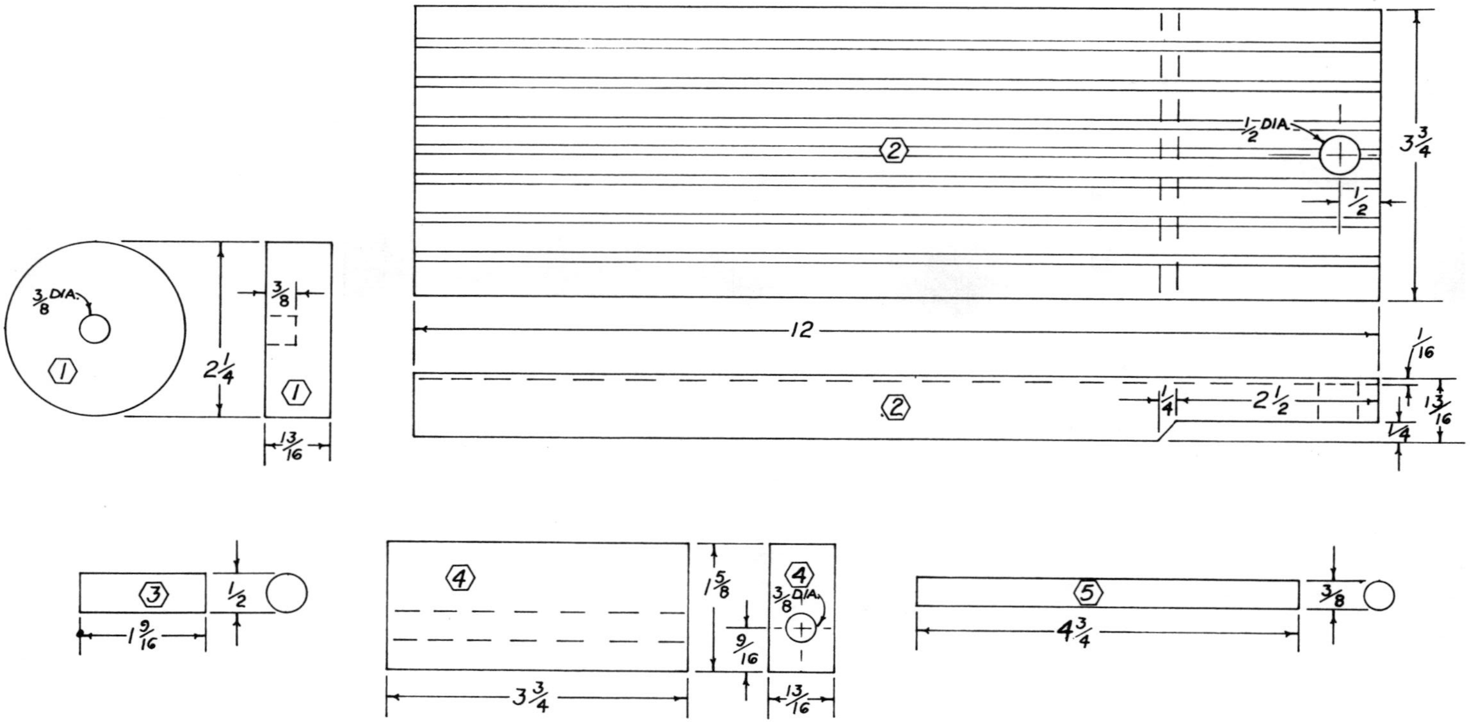

·17·
Pirate's Cannon

Figure 17–1

The Pirate's Cannon can be either a toy or a conversation
piece. Scaling up the size of the cannon will increase interest
as a decorative item.

PART	DIMENSIONS (thickness x width x length)	QUANTITY
1. Cannon Barrel	3 dia. x 18	1
2. Hinge Pivot Shaft	1 dia. x $3\frac{1}{4}$	2
3. Hinge Clamp	$\frac{7}{8}$ x $\frac{13}{16}$ x $3\frac{13}{16}$	2
4. Side	$\frac{13}{16}$ x 6 x $12\frac{1}{2}$	2
5. Axle	$\frac{1}{2}$ dia. x $8\frac{1}{4}$	2
6. Wheel	$1\frac{5}{8}$ x 4 dia.	4
7. Base	$\frac{13}{16}$ x $5\frac{5}{8}$ x $12\frac{1}{2}$	1
8. Front Brace	$\frac{13}{16}$ x 3 x $5\frac{5}{8}$	1
9. Rear Brace	$\frac{13}{16}$ x $2\frac{3}{16}$ x $5\frac{5}{8}$	1

Construction

1. Redraw the Pirate's Cannon patterns to full scale, using the dimensions shown in Figures 17–4, 17–5, and 17–6.
2. Select the amount of clean, blemish-free hardwood stock needed to complete the Pirate's Cannon.
3. If not already milled, mill the rough 1″ woodstock to $\frac{13}{16}$″ thickness.
4. Laminate enough $\frac{13}{16}$″ woodstock to achieve the desired thickness or use 2″ woodstock for the cannon barrel 1 and wheels 6. Glue and clamp the wood together and allow to dry.
5. Prepare the production patterns as needed. Label for future use.
6. Place the milled woodstock on a worktable and draw or trace all of the Pirate's Cannon parts onto it.
7. For easier handling, cut the hardwood to rough lengths approximately 8″ long on the radial arm saw. Be careful not to cut through a toy part during this process.
8. Joint the edges of the milled woodstock on the jointer to give a straight edge to guide future cuts on the table saw and radial arm saw.
9. On the table saw or radial arm saw, cut the following parts to the exact rectangular dimensions listed previously.
   - 1 Cannon Barrel
   - 3 Hinge Clamps
   - 4 Sides
   - 7 Base
   - 8 Front Brace
   - 9 Rear Brace
10. Cut the following parts out on the band saw. One-inch dowel is recommended for the hinge pivot shaft 2, in which case it and the axles need only be cut to length.
    - 2 Hinge Pivot Shaft
    - 3 Hinge Clamps
    - 4 Sides (steps only)
    - 5 Axles
    - 6 Wheels

When cutting on the band saw, do not cut into the pencil lines. Allow a little excess wood to remain outside the lines so that final shaping can be done on the disc sander.

11. Disc sand the following parts to shape.
    5 Axles (taper ends slightly)
    6 Wheels

12. Drill suitably sized holes into the following parts. See drawings for details.
    1 Cannon Barrel (1″ hinge pivot shaft hole; 1¼″ barrel shaft)
    6 Wheels (axle holes)
    7 Base (axle hole)
    4 Sides (axle holes)

13. Belt sand the hinge clamp 3 to size and shape. Use a 1″ belt sander.

14. Square the ends of the woodstock that is to be turned on the lathe for the cannon barrel. Place the rough woodstock for the cannon barrel on the lathe and turn it to desired shape. See drawings for details.

15. Belt sand all of the flat surfaces to a smooth finish, sanding with the grain to prevent scratches.

16. Remove all sharp edges and corners using a router or sandpaper.

Assembly

Note: For how to glue and dowel parts together, see the procedure described in the Introduction.

1. Glue and dowel the sides 4 to the base 7, making sure first that the axle holes of the sides and base are in alignment.

2. Glue and dowel the front brace 8 and rear brace 9 to the sides 4 and base 7. See drawings for details.

3. Glue the hinge pivot shaft 2 to the cannon barrel 1 hinge holes that were drilled on the side of the barrel. See drawings for details.

4. Place the cannon barrel 1 and hinge pivot shaft 2 into the cannon frame and then glue and dowel the hinge clamps 3 to the sides 4. See drawings for details.

5. Place the axles 5 into the base 7 axle holes, and then glue the wheels 6 to the axles 5.

6. Sand the surface of the Pirate's Cannon to remove scratches and blemishes.

7. Apply one or two coats of boiled linseed oil to the surface.

Figure 17–2 Top view of Pirate's Cannon.

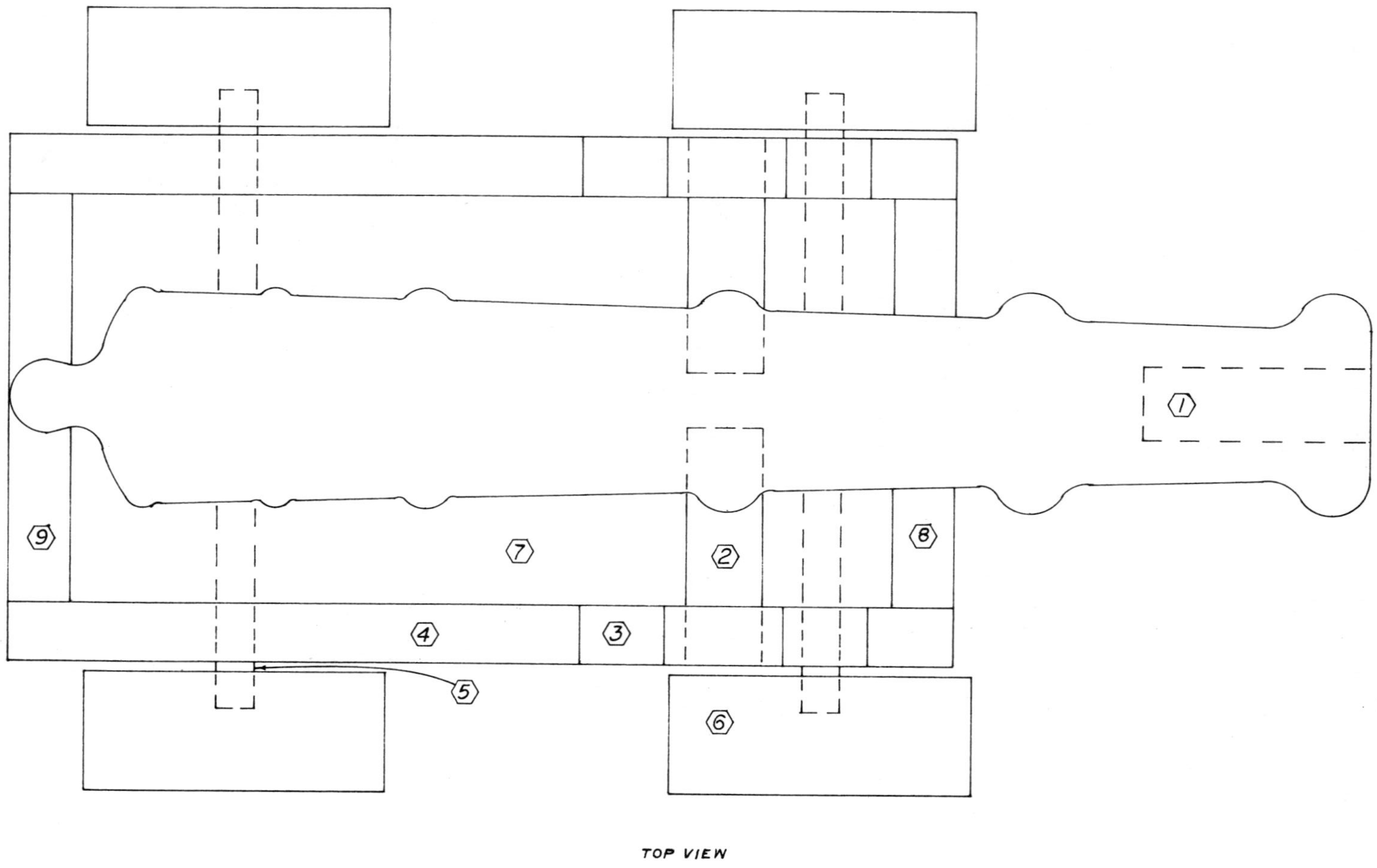

TOP VIEW

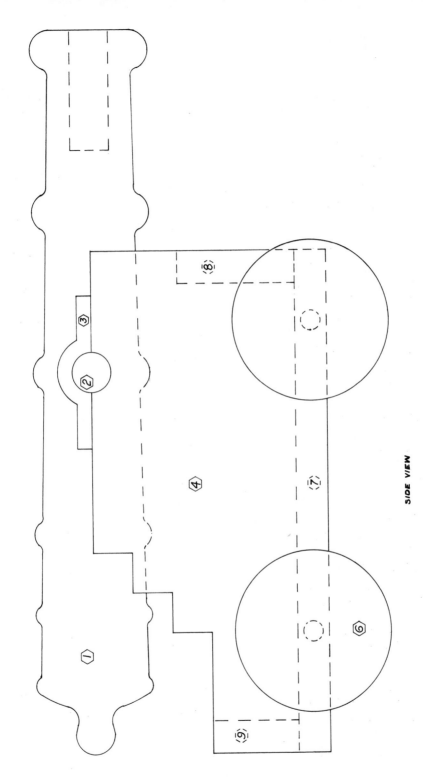

SIDE VIEW

Figure 17-3 Side view of Pirate's Cannon.

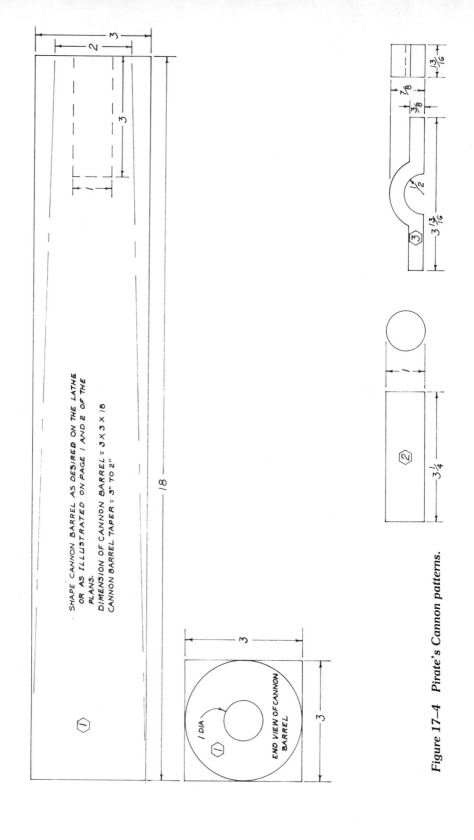

SHAPE CANNON BARREL AS DESIRED ON THE LATHE OR AS ILLUSTRATED ON PAGE 1 AND 2 OF THE PLANS.
DIMENSION OF CANNON BARREL = 3 X 3 X 18
CANNON BARREL TAPER = 3" TO 2"

END VIEW OF CANNON BARREL

I DIA

Figure 17–4 Pirate's Cannon patterns.

108

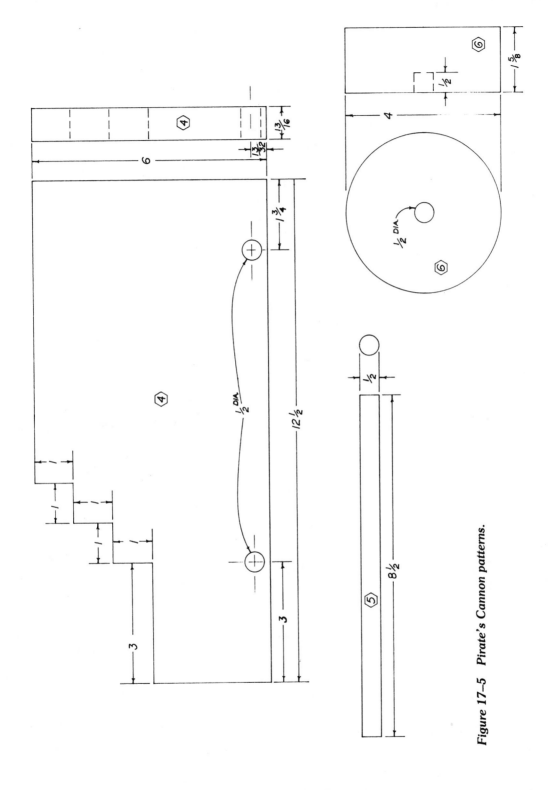

Figure 17-5 Pirate's Cannon patterns.

109

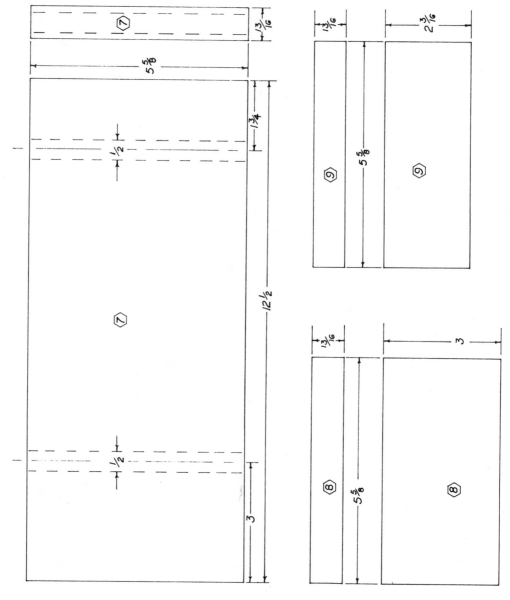

Figure 17–6 Pirate's Cannon patterns.

·18·
Mini Bus

Figure 18–1

A child can take lovely mini vacations with his or her own miniature RV.

PART	DIMENSIONS (thickness x width x length)	QUANTITY
1. Roof	$\frac{13}{16}$ x 4 x $8\frac{1}{2}$	1
2. Sides	$\frac{13}{16}$ x $4\frac{3}{4}$ x $7\frac{3}{4}$	2 (R & L)
3. Front	$\frac{9}{16}$ x 4 x $3\frac{1}{4}$	1
4. Grill	$\frac{13}{16}$ x $1\frac{1}{2}$ x 4	1
5. Wheel	$1\frac{5}{8}$ x 2 dia.	4
6. Base	$\frac{13}{16}$ x $2\frac{3}{8}$ x $7\frac{3}{4}$	1
7. Bumper	$\frac{1}{2}$ x $\frac{1}{2}$ x $4\frac{1}{2}$	1
8. Axle	$\frac{3}{8}$ dia. x $3\frac{5}{8}$	2

Construction

1. Redraw the Mini Bus patterns to full scale, using the dimensions shown in Figures 18–3 and 18–4.
2. Select the amount of clean, blemish-free hardwood stock needed to complete the Mini Bus.
3. If not already milled, mill the rough 1″ woodstock to $\frac{13}{16}$″ thickness.
4. Prepare the production patterns as needed. Label each for later use.
5. Place the milled woodstock on a worktable and draw or trace all of the bus parts onto it.
6. To make handling easier, cut the hardwood into rough lengths approximately 8″ long on the radial arm saw. Be sure not to cut through any toy parts.
7. Joint the edges of the milled woodstock on the jointer. This provides a straight edge to guide future cuts on the table saw and radial arm saw.
8. On the table saw or radial arm saw, cut the following parts to the exact rectangular dimensions listed previously.

   [1] Roof
   [2] Sides (also cut side angles; note that you can have two windows, as provided in plans, or three—as shown in Figure 18–1)
   [3] Front (also cut to $\frac{9}{16}$″ thickness)
   [4] Grill (also make the slant cut)
   [6] Base
   [7] Bumper

9. Cut the wheels [5] out on the band saw, leaving some excess wood outside the pencil lines so that final shaping can be done on the disc sander.
10. With the drill press and circle saws, drill the windows and fender wells into the right and left sides [2] of the Mini Bus. See drawings for details.
11. Drill the axle holes into the wheels [5] and base [6]. See drawings for details.
12. Disc sand the wheels [5] to size and shape.
13. Remove all of the sharp edges and corners with the router or sandpaper.
14. Belt sand all of the flat surfaces to remove scratches and blemishes. Always sand with the grain to avoid scratching the wood.

Assembly

1. Glue and dowel the following parts together, following the procedure described in the Introduction. Use any sequence that seems convenient.

   1 Roof   4 Grill
   2 Sides   6 Base
   3 Front   7 Bumper

2. Place the axles 8 into the base 6 axle holes, and then glue the wheels 5 to the axles 8.

3. Sand the surface of the Mini Bus to remove scratches and blemishes.

4. Apply one or two coats of boiled linseed oil to finish the surface of the bus.

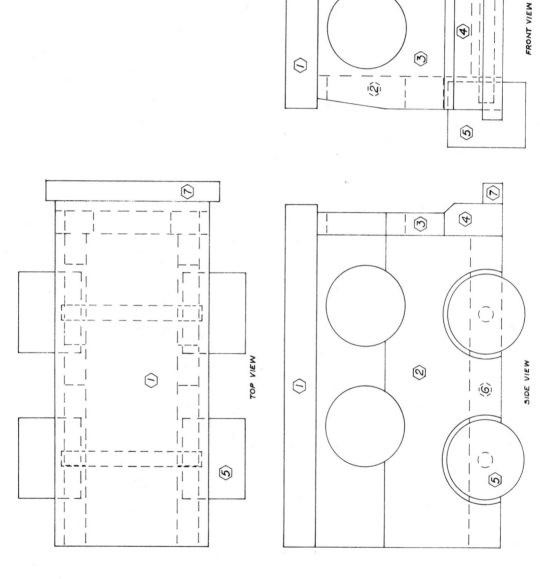

Figure 18-2   Top, side, and front views of the Mini Bus.

TOP VIEW

SIDE VIEW

FRONT VIEW

114

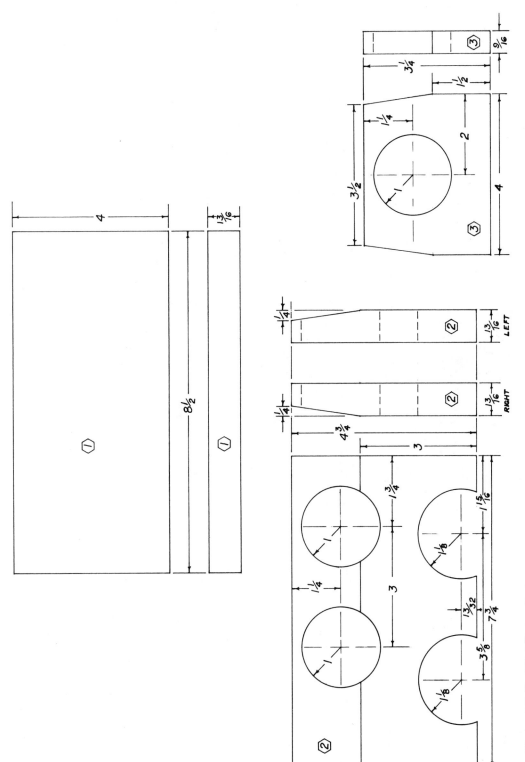

Figure 18–3 Mini Bus patterns.

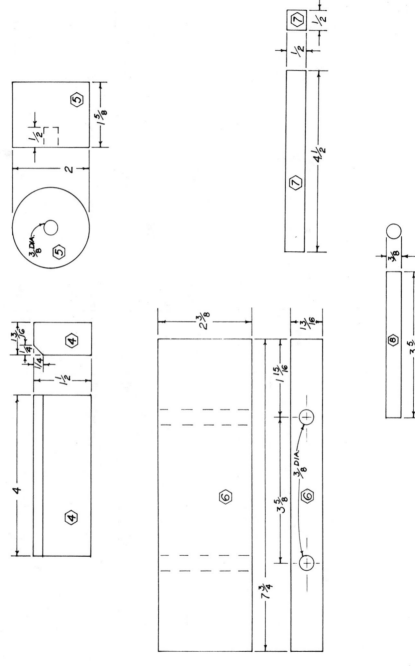

Figure 18–4 Mini Bus patterns.

116

·19·
The Wooden Chicken

Figure 19–1

The Wooden Chicken is clean and quiet—an ideal pet.
It is also easy to make, and several of them can be built in a
short period of time.

PART	DIMENSIONS (thickness x width x length)	QUANTITY
1. Body	$\frac{13}{16}$ x 5 x $5\frac{7}{8}$	1
2. Wheel	$\frac{13}{16}$ x 3 dia.	4
3. Axle	$\frac{3}{8}$ dia. x $1\frac{11}{16}$	2
4. Comb (red felt)	As desired	1

Construction

1. Redraw The Wooden Chicken patterns to full scale, using the dimensions shown in Figure 19–3.
2. Select the amount of clean, blemish-free hardwood stock needed to complete the project.
3. If not already milled, mill the rough 1″ woodstock to $\frac{13}{16}$″ thickness.
4. Prepare the production patterns as needed. Label each for later use.
5. Place the milled woodstock on a worktable and draw or trace all of The Wooden Chicken parts onto it.
6. Cut the hardwood to easy-to-handle lengths on the radial arm saw, being careful not to cut through any toy parts.
7. Joint the edges of the milled woodstock on the jointer. This gives a flat edge to guide future cuts on the table saw and radial arm saw.
8. Cut the body ☐1 of the chicken to the required width and length on the table saw or radial arm saw. Cut the groove for the comb at this time also. This cut should be made before the slanted cut for the chicken's back is made. See the drawings for details.
9. Shape the body ☐1 and wheels ☐2 on the band saw. Allow some excess wood to remain outside the pencil lines so that finishing can be done on the disc sander.
10. Drill the eye hole into the body ☐1 and axle holes into the wheels ☐2. See drawings for details.
11. Disc sand the body and wheels to size and shape.
12. Belt sand all of the flat surfaces to remove scratches and blemishes.
13. Remove all of the sharp edges and corners with router or sandpaper.

Assembly

1. Place the axles ☐3 into the axle holes of the body ☐1 and then glue the wheels ☐2 to the axles ☐3.
2. Cut the comb to the desired shape and glue it in the groove in the head of the body ☐1.
3. If desired, apply one or two coats of boiled linseed oil as a finish.

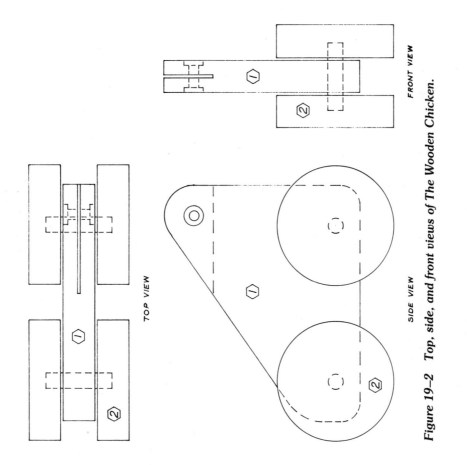

TOP VIEW

FRONT VIEW

SIDE VIEW

Figure 19-2   Top, side, and front views of The Wooden Chicken.

119

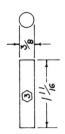

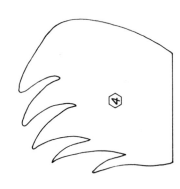

DESIGN COMB AS DESIRED
USE RED FELT CLOTH
PLACE COMB INTO 1/16" SLOT CUT IN HEAD

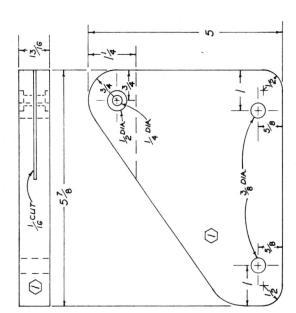

Figure 19–3   The Wooden Chicken patterns.

·20·
Fork Lift

Figure 20–1

Blocks and boxes are now easier to move from place
to place with the aid of the Fork Lift. The moveable forks
allow objects to be placed on trailers.

PART	DIMENSIONS (thickness x width x length)	QUANTITY
1. Cab Top	$\frac{13}{16}$ x $4\frac{5}{8}$ x 8	1
2. Engine Hood	$\frac{13}{16}$ x $4\frac{5}{8}$ x $2\frac{3}{4}$	1
3. Weight Support	$\frac{13}{16}$ x $4\frac{5}{8}$ x $3\frac{1}{2}$	1
4. Weight Support	$\frac{13}{16}$ x $4\frac{5}{8}$ x 5	1
5. Floor	$\frac{13}{16}$ x $4\frac{5}{8}$ x 8	1
6. Side	$\frac{13}{16}$ x $2\frac{3}{4}$ x 8	2 (R & L)
7. Wheel	$1\frac{5}{8}$ x 3 dia.	4
8. Floor Brace	$\frac{13}{16}$ x $1\frac{15}{16}$ x 3	2
9. Slide	$\frac{3}{4}$ x $\frac{3}{4}$ x $6\frac{1}{2}$	2
10. Carriage Slide Frame	$\frac{1}{2}$ x $\frac{3}{4}$ x 7	2
11. Bottom Slide Brace	$\frac{1}{2}$ x $\frac{3}{4}$ x $4\frac{5}{8}$	1
12. Fork	$\frac{1}{2}$ x $\frac{3}{4}$ x 4	2
13. Foot Rest	1 x 1 x $4\frac{5}{8}$	1
14. Front Cab Post	$\frac{3}{8}$ dia. x $5\frac{3}{8}$	2
15. Steering Wheel	$\frac{13}{16}$ x $1\frac{1}{2}$ dia.	1
16. Steering Post	$\frac{3}{8}$ dia. x 2	1
17. Seat Back	$\frac{1}{2}$ x 2 x $4\frac{5}{8}$	1
18. Base	$\frac{13}{16}$ x 3 x 8	1
19. Axle	$\frac{3}{8}$ dia. x $4\frac{1}{4}$	2
20. Rear Cab Post	$\frac{3}{8}$ dia. x $6\frac{1}{8}$	2
21. Slide Rail	$\frac{13}{16}$ x 1 x $5\frac{5}{8}$	2
22. Carriage Braces	$\frac{1}{2}$ x $\frac{3}{4}$ x 5	3
23. Bottom Carriage Brace	$\frac{1}{2}$ x $\frac{3}{4}$ x 5	1
24. Slide Rail Brace	$\frac{1}{2}$ x $\frac{13}{16}$ x $1\frac{7}{8}$	3

Construction

1. Redraw the Fork Lift patterns to full scale, using the dimensions shown in Figures 20–5 through 20–8.
2. Select the amount of clean, blemish-free hardwood stock needed to complete the Fork Lift.
3. If not already milled, mill the rough 1″ woodstock to $\frac{13}{16}$″ thickness. Laminate $\frac{13}{16}$″ to desired thickness for wheels or use 2″ woodstock.
4. Prepare the production patterns as needed. Label each pattern for later use.
5. Place the milled woodstock on a worktable and draw or trace all of the Fork Lift parts onto it.
6. Cut the hardwood into easy-to-handle lengths on the radial arm saw. Be careful not to cut through any toy parts during this process.
7. To provide a straight edge to guide future cuts, joint the edges of the milled woodstock on the jointer.

8. On the table saw or radial arm saw, cut the following parts to the exact rectangular dimensions listed previously.

[1]	Cab Top	[11]	Bottom Slide Brace
[2]	Engine Hood	[12]	Forks
[3]	Weight Support	[13]	Foot Rest
[4]	Weight Support	[17]	Seat Back
[5]	Floor	[18]	Base
[6]	Sides	[21]	Slide Rail
[8]	Floor Braces	[22]	Carriage Braces
[9]	Slides	[23]	Bottom Carriage Brace
[10]	Carriage Slide Frames	[24]	Slide Rail Brace

9. Cut dado cuts into the following parts. See the drawings for details.

[9] Slide
[21] Slide Rail
[23] Bottom Carriage Brace

10. Cut the following parts out on the band saw, leaving a small amount of excess wood outside the pencil lines so final shaping can be done on the disc sander.

[2]	Engine Hood	[16]	Steering Post
[6]	Sides (fender wells)	[19]	Axles
[7]	Wheels	[20]	Rear Cab Posts
[14]	Front Cab Posts		

11. Drill axle holes and post holes into the following parts.

[4]	Weight (post holes)	[7]	Wheels (axle holes)
[5]	Floor (post holes)	[18]	Base (axle holes)

12. Shape the following parts on the disc and drum sanders.

[2] Engine hood
[6] Sides (drum sand the fender wells)
[7] Wheels

13. Belt sand all of the flat surfaces of the Fork Lift to remove scratches and blemishes. Sand with the grain to avoid scratching the wood.

14. Do the final shaping of the following parts on the disc sander.

[13] Foot Rest (slant)
[17] Seat Back

Assembly

Note: For how to glue and dowel parts together, see the procedure described in the Introduction.

1. Glue and dowel the following parts together to form the Fork Lift body.

[5]	Floor	[8]	Floor Braces
[6]	Sides	[18]	Base

2. Glue and dowel the following parts together to form the "slide section".

[9]	Slides	[12]	Forks
[10]	Carriage Slide Frames	[22]	Carriage Braces
[11]	Bottom Slide Brace		

3. Glue and dowel the following parts to the Fork Lift body.

   2̲ Engine Hood   4̲ Weight Support

   3̲ Weight Support   17̲ Seat Back

4. Glue and dowel the remaining parts to the Fork Lift, using any convenient sequence. See drawings for details.

5. Place the axles 19̲ in the axle holes of the base 18̲ and then glue the wheels 7̲ to the axles 19̲.

6. Sand the surface of the Fork Lift to remove scratches and blemishes.

7. To finish the surface, apply one or two coats of boiled linseed oil.

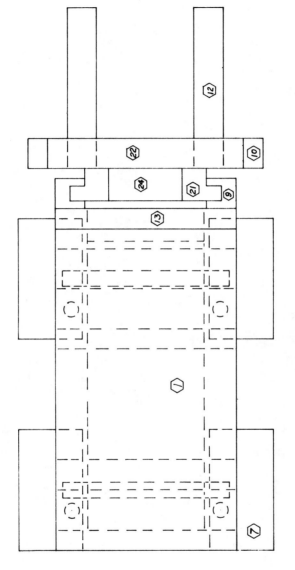

TOP VIEW

Figure 20–2 Top view of the Fork Lift.

Figure 20–3   Side view of the Fork Lift.

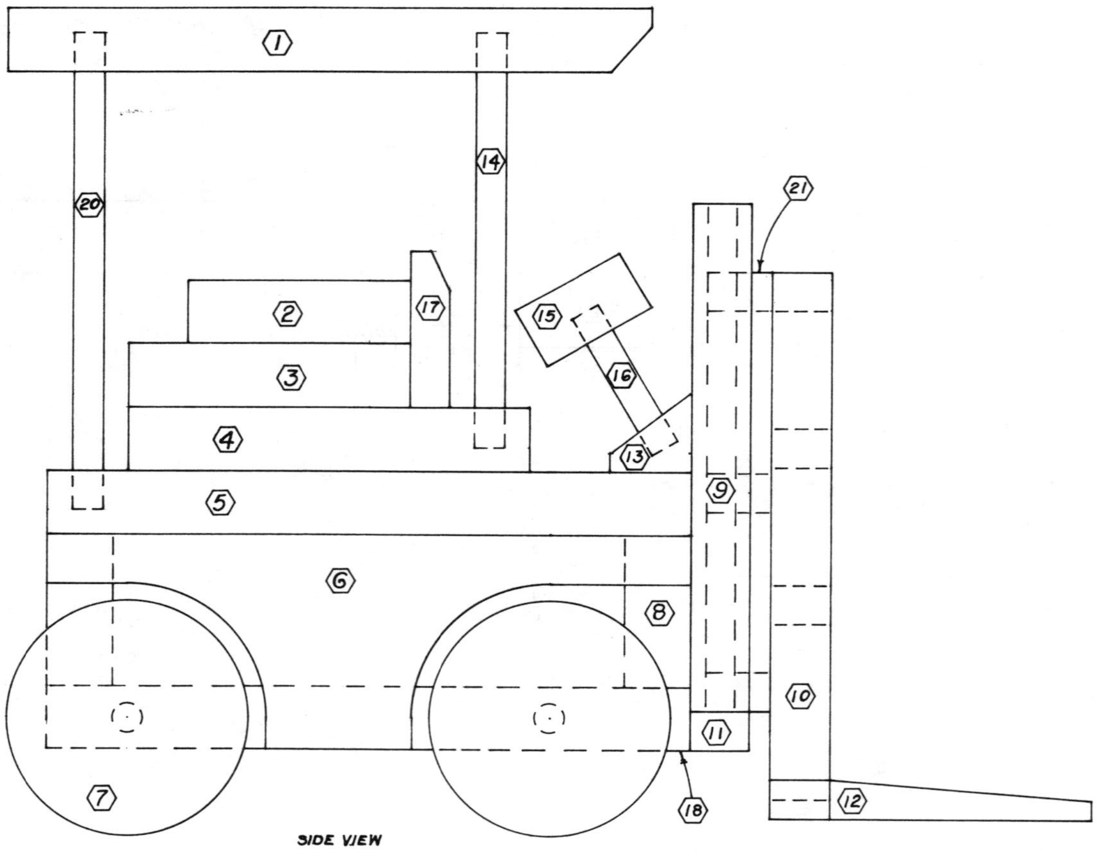

SIDE VIEW

126

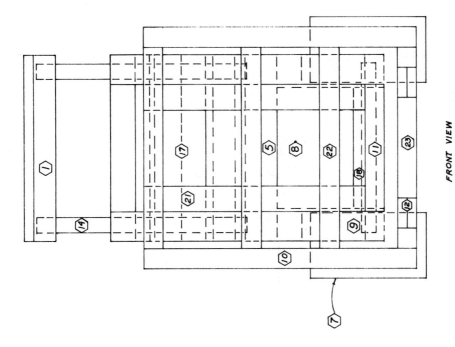

FRONT VIEW

Figure 20—4 Front view of the Fork Lift.

127

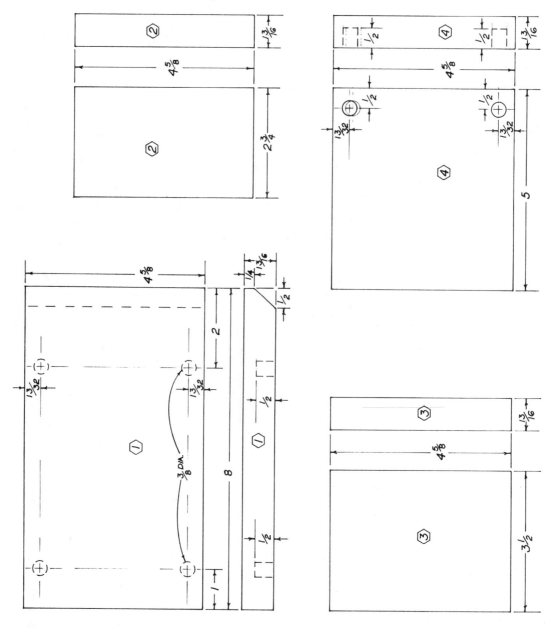

Figure 20-5 Fork Lift patterns.

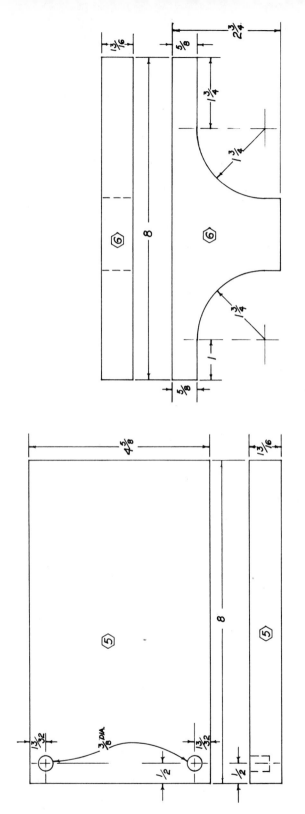

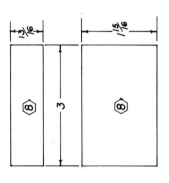

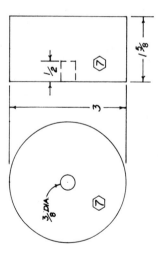

Figure 20–6 Fork Lift patterns.

129

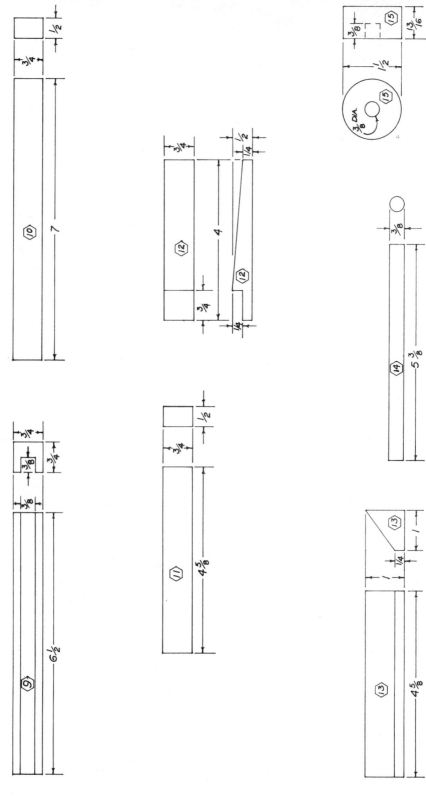

Figure 20–7 Fork Lift patterns.

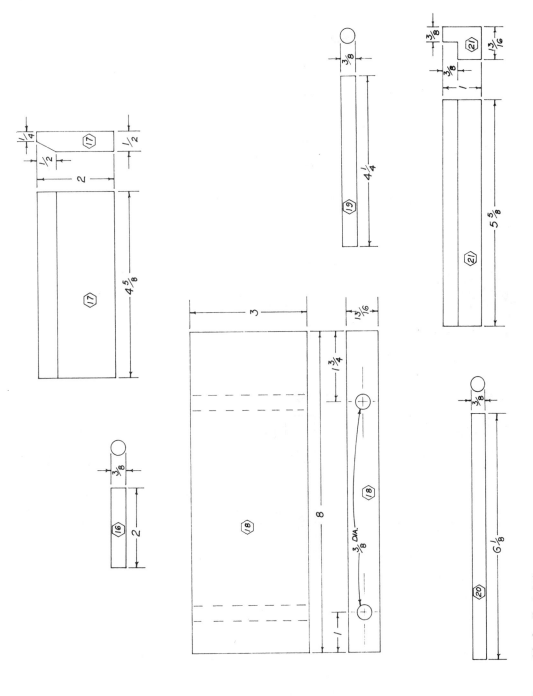

Figure 20–8   Fork Lift patterns.

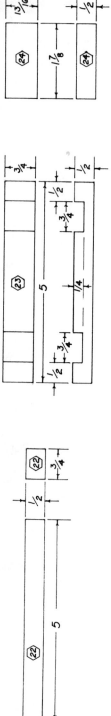

Figure 20–9 Fork Lift patterns.

·21·
Pick-Up Truck

Figure 21–1
From left: Train Engine, Pick-Up Truck, Goose Neck Trailer hauling Tractor.

A pick-up truck is an indispensable vehicle—
for work or for play.

PART	DIMENSIONS (thickness x width x length)	QUANTITY
1. Cab Roof	$\frac{13}{16}$ x $3\frac{3}{16}$ x $4\frac{5}{8}$	1
2. Body Side	$\frac{13}{16}$ x $4\frac{5}{8}$ x 11	2
3. Engine Hood	$\frac{13}{16}$ x $2\frac{1}{2}$ x $4\frac{5}{8}$	1
4. Grill	$\frac{13}{16}$ x 2 x $4\frac{5}{8}$	1
5. Bumper	$\frac{1}{2}$ x $\frac{13}{16}$ x $5\frac{5}{8}$	2
6. Wheel	$1\frac{5}{8}$ x $2\frac{1}{2}$ dia.	4
7. Base	$\frac{13}{16}$ x 3 x 11	1
8. Tail Gate	$\frac{13}{16}$ x $2\frac{1}{2}$ x 3	1
9. Axle Housing	$\frac{13}{16}$ x 2 x 3	2
10. Axle	$\frac{3}{8}$ dia. x $4\frac{1}{4}$	2
11. Trailer Hitch	$\frac{13}{16}$ x 2 x 3	1

Construction

1. Redraw the Pick-Up Truck patterns to full scale, using the dimensions shown in Figures 21–4 and 21–5.
2. Select the amount of clean, blemish-free hardwood stock needed to complete the Pick-Up Truck.
3. If not already milled, mill the rough 1″ woodstock to $\frac{13}{16}$″ thickness.
4. Prepare the production patterns as needed. Label each pattern for later use.
5. Place the milled woodstock on a worktable and draw or trace all of the Pick-Up Truck parts onto it.
6. Cut the hardwood into easy-to-handle lengths on the radial arm saw, being careful not to cut through any toy parts.
7. Joint the edges of the milled woodstock on the jointer. This provides a straight edge to guide future cuts on the table saw and radial arm saw.
8. On the table saw or radial arm saw, cut the following parts to the exact rectangular dimensions listed previously.
   - 1 Cab Roof (also cut the angle)
   - 2 Body Sides
   - 3 Engine Hood (also cut the angle)
   - 4 Grill
   - 5 Bumper
   - 7 Base
   - 8 Tail Gate
   - 9 Axle Housing
   - 11 Trailer Hitch
9. Cut out the windows in the body sides 2 on the drill press with the aid of a circle saw. See the drawings for details.
10. Cut the following parts to shape on the band saw.
    - 2 Body Sides (cut out fender wells)
    - 6 Wheels
    - 10 Axles

Do not cut into the pencil lines. Allow a small amount of excess wood to remain outside the lines so that final shaping can be done on the disc sander and belt sander.

11. Drill axle holes and other holes into the following parts. See the drawings for details.
    - 6 Wheels (axle holes)
    - 9 Axle Housing (axle hole)
    - 11 Trailer Hitch

12. Shape the following parts on the disc sander, 1″ belt sander, 6″ belt sander, and drum sander.
    - 2 Body Sides (drum sand the fender wells)
    - 6 Wheels

13. Belt sand all of the flat surfaces to remove scratches and blemishes, sanding with the grain of the wood.

14. Remove all sharp edges and corners.

Assembly

Note: For how to glue and dowel parts together, see the procedure described in the Introduction.

1. Glue and dowel the following parts together to form the body of the Pick-Up Truck.
   - 1 Cab Roof
   - 2 Body Sides
   - 3 Engine Hood
   - 4 Grill
   - 5 Bumpers
   - 7 Base
   - 8 Tail Gate
   - 9 Axle Housing

2. Glue and dowel the trailer hitch 11 to the base 7. See the drawings for details.

3. Place the axles 10 into the axle holes of the base 7 and then glue the wheels 6 to the axles 10.

4. Sand the surface of the Pick-Up Truck to remove scratches and blemishes.

5. Apply one or two coats of boiled linseed oil to the surface of the truck.

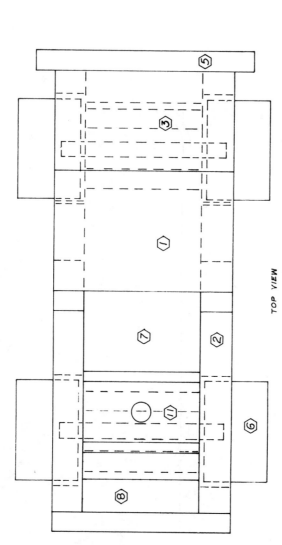

Figure 21–2   Top and front views of the Pick-Up Truck.

TOP VIEW

FRONT VIEW

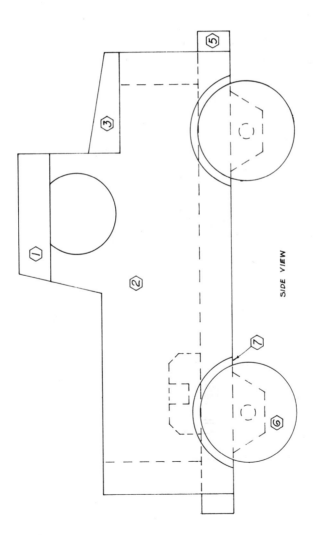

SIDE VIEW

Figure 21—3   Side view of the Pick-Up Truck.

Figure 21–4 Pick-Up Truck patterns.

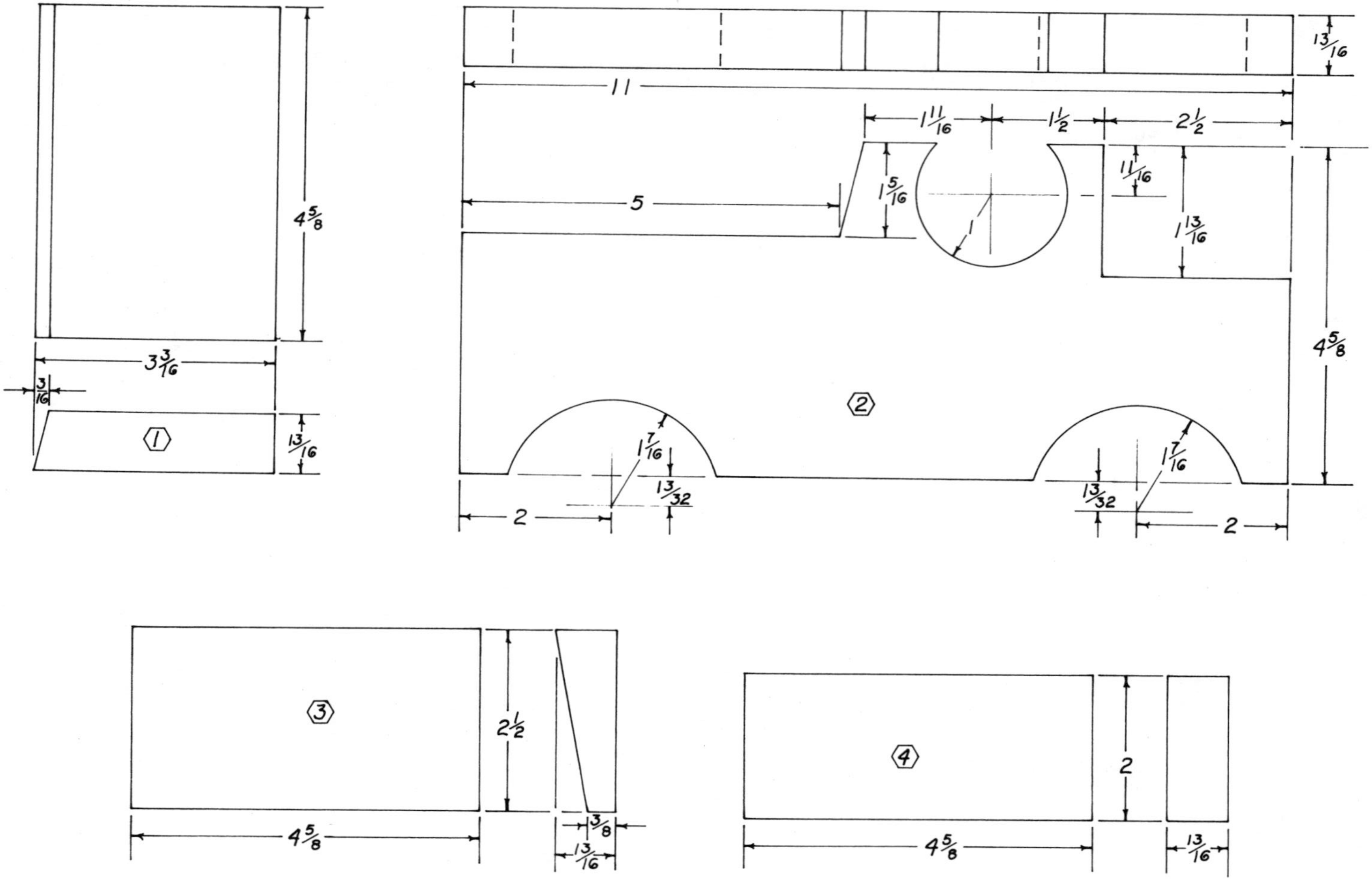

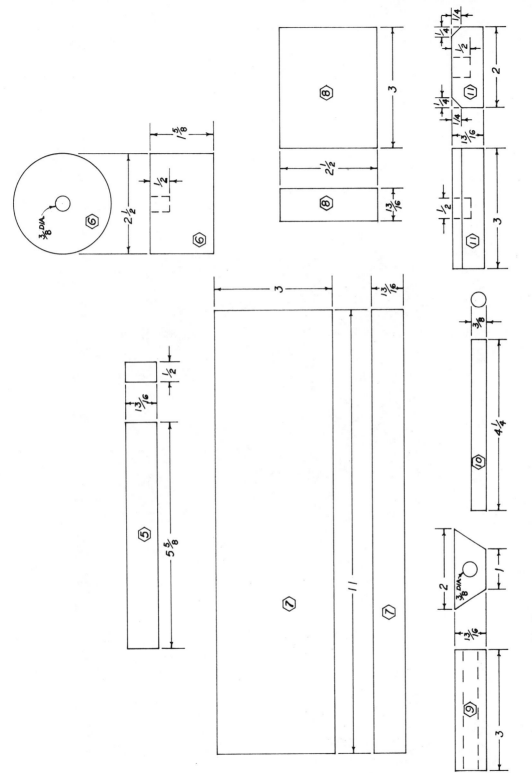

Figure 21–5 Pick-Up Truck patterns.

·22·

Goose Neck Trailer

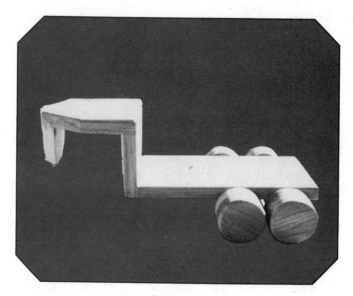

Figure 22–1

The goose neck trailer is a very versatile piece of
equipment on the farm as well as in a small industry.
Its quick means of attachment adds to its convenience as
well as ease of handling on the road.

PART	DIMENSIONS (thickness x width x length)	QUANTITY
1. Top	$\frac{13}{16} \times 4\frac{5}{8} \times 5\frac{5}{8}$	1
2. Back	$\frac{13}{16} \times 4\frac{5}{8} \times 3\frac{3}{4}$	1
3. Tongue	$\frac{13}{16} \times 2\frac{3}{8} \times 2\frac{1}{4}$	1
4. Bed	$\frac{13}{16} \times 4\frac{5}{8} \times 10$	1
5. Wheel	$1\frac{5}{8} \times 2\frac{1}{2}$ dia.	4
6. Axle Housing	$\frac{13}{16} \times 2 \times 4\frac{5}{8}$	2
7. Hitch	$\frac{1}{2}$ dia. $\times 1\frac{1}{4}$	1
8. Axle	$\frac{3}{8}$ dia. $\times 5\frac{5}{8}$	2

Construction

1. Redraw the Goose Neck Trailer patterns to full scale, using the dimensions shown in Figures 22–4 and 22–5.
2. Select the amount of clean, blemish-free hardwood stock needed to complete the trailer.
3. If not already milled, mill the rough 1″ woodstock to $\frac{13}{16}$″ thickness. Laminate $\frac{13}{16}$″ woodstock to desired thickness for wheels or use 2″ woodstock.
4. Prepare the production patterns as needed. Label each for later use.
5. Place the milled woodstock on a worktable and draw or trace all of the Goose Neck Trailer parts onto it.
6. For easier handling, cut the hardwood into pieces approximately 8″ long or longer on the radial arm saw. Be sure not to cut through any of the toy parts in the process.
7. Joint the edges of the milled woodstock on the jointer to give a straight edge to guide future cuts on the table saw and radial arm saw.
8. On the table saw or radial arm saw, cut the following parts to the exact rectangular dimensions listed previously.
   [1] Top (also cut the angles)
   [2] Back
   [3] Tongue (also cut the angles)
   [4] Bed (also cut the grooves)
   [6] Axle Housing
9. Drill the axle holes and hitch hole into the following parts.
   [3] Tongue (hitch hole)
   [5] Wheels (axle holes)
   [6] Axle Housings (axle holes)
10. Cut the following parts to size on the band saw, allowing a small amount of wood to remain beyond the pencil lines so that final shaping can be done on the disc sander and belt sander.
    [5] Wheels
    [8] Axles
11. On the disc sander, shape the wheels [5] and taper the ends of the hitch [7] and axles [8].

12. Belt sand all of the flat surfaces of the Goose Neck Trailer, sanding with the grain to avoid scratching the wood.
13. Smooth all sharp edges and corners.

Assembly

1. Glue and dowel the following parts together to form the trailer.
   1. Top
   2. Back
   3. Tongue
   4. Bed
   6. Axle Housing
2. Place the axles 8 into the axle housings 6 and then glue the wheels 5 to the axles 8.
3. Sand the surface of the Goose Neck Trailer to remove scratches and blemishes.
4. For a wood finish, apply one or two coats of boiled linseed oil.

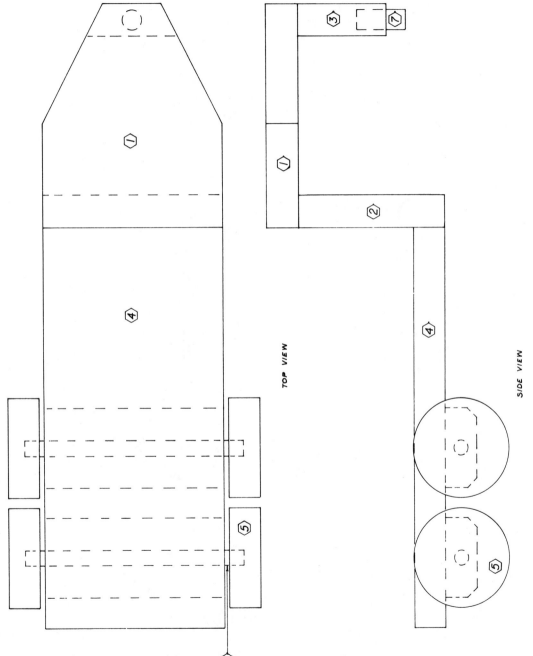

TOP VIEW

SIDE VIEW

Figure 22–2 Top and side views of the Goose Neck Trailer.

143

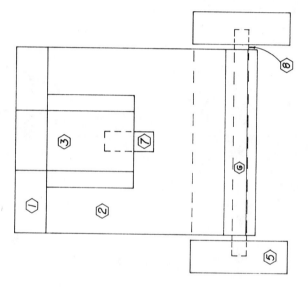

FRONT VIEW

Figure 22–3 Front view of the Goose Neck Trailer.

144

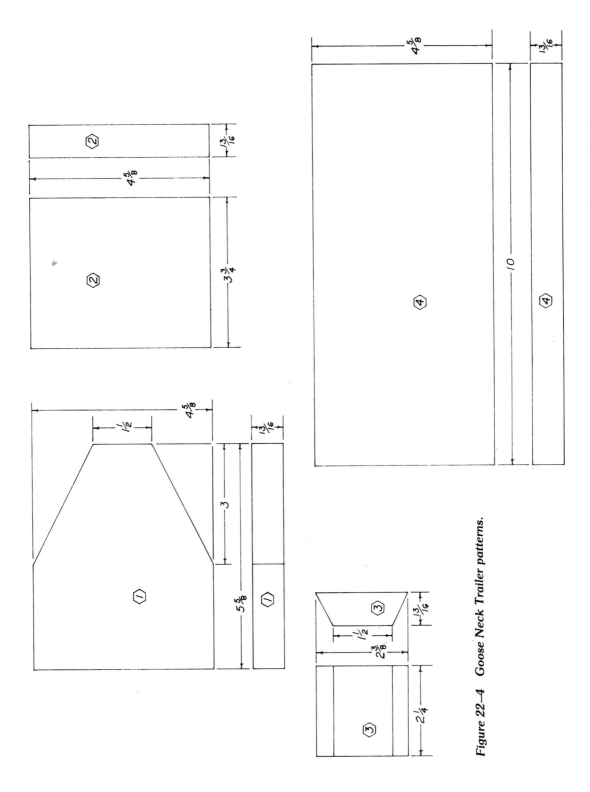

Figure 22-4 Goose Neck Trailer patterns.

145

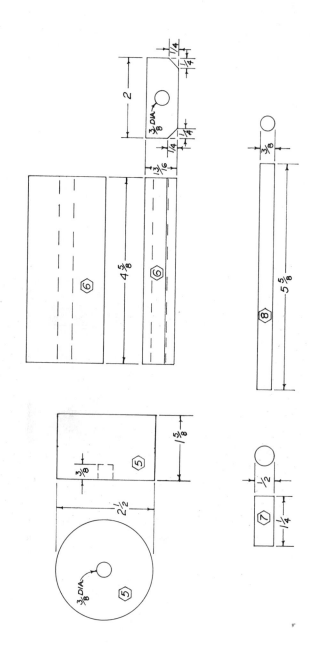

Figure 22–5 Goose Neck Trailer patterns.

·23·

Tri-Pod Truck

Figure 23–1

Conventional trucks have at least four tires and wheels.
The Tri-Pod Truck has only three, saving money and materials.
This type of vehicle is used on farms to spread commercial
fertilizer. The tires are the huge balloon type, and
when observed in action, the truck appears to be bouncing
across the field.

PART	DIMENSIONS (thickness x width x length)	QUANTITY
1. Cab Roof	$\frac{13}{16}$ x $2\frac{3}{4}$ x $3\frac{1}{2}$	1
2. Cab Post	$\frac{13}{16}$ x $\frac{13}{16}$ x $1\frac{1}{2}$	4
3. Engine Hood	$\frac{13}{16}$ x $3\frac{1}{2}$ x $4\frac{9}{16}$	1
4. Tri-Pod Top	$\frac{13}{16}$ $2\frac{7}{8}$ x $3\frac{1}{2}$	1
5. Tri-Pod Leg	$\frac{13}{16}$ x $1\frac{13}{16}$ x $2\frac{7}{8}$	2
6. Wheel	$1\frac{5}{8}$ x $2\frac{1}{2}$ dia.	3
7. Cab Side	$\frac{13}{16}$ x $1\frac{7}{8}$ x $2\frac{3}{4}$	2
8. Base	$\frac{13}{16}$ x $3\frac{1}{2}$ x $7\frac{3}{4}$	1
9. Bed Front and Rear	$\frac{13}{16}$ x $3\frac{1}{2}$ x $7\frac{7}{8}$	1 each
10. Gas Tank	$\frac{13}{16}$ x 1 x 2	2
11. Bed Sides	$\frac{13}{16}$ x $3\frac{1}{2}$ x $4\frac{7}{16}$	2 (R & L)
12. Fender	$\frac{13}{16}$ x $2\frac{1}{4}$ x $4\frac{7}{8}$	2 (R & L)
13. Rear Fender	$\frac{3}{8}$ x $\frac{3}{4}$ x $5\frac{1}{2}$	1
14. Spreader	$\frac{13}{16}$ x 1 x 2	1
15. Rear Bumper	$\frac{3}{8}$ x $\frac{13}{16}$ x $5\frac{1}{2}$	1
16. Bed Bottom	$\frac{13}{16}$ x $2\frac{3}{4}$ x $3\frac{1}{2}$	1
17. Front Axle	$\frac{3}{8}$ dia. x $2\frac{7}{8}$	1
18. Rear Axle	$\frac{3}{8}$ dia. x $4\frac{3}{8}$	1

Construction

1. Redraw the Tri-Pod Truck patterns to full scale, using the dimensions shown in Figures 23–5 through 23–7.
2. Select the amount of clean, blemish-free hardwood stock needed to complete the Tri-Pod Truck.
3. If not already milled, mill the rough 1″ woodstock to $\frac{13}{16}$″ thickness.
4. Prepare the production patterns as needed. Label each pattern for later use.
5. Place the milled woodstock on a worktable and draw or trace all of the Tri-Pod Truck parts onto it.
6. Cut the hardwood into easy-to-handle lengths on the radial arm saw, being careful not to cut through any toy parts.
7. Joint the edges of the milled woodstock on the jointer to give a straight edge for guiding future cuts on the table saw and radial arm saw.
8. On the table saw or radial arm saw, cut the following parts to the exact rectangular dimensions listed previously.

   1 Cab Roof
   2 Cab Post
   3 Engine Hood
   4 Tri-Pod Top
   5 Tri-Pod Leg

   7 Cab Side
   8 Base
   9 Bed Front and Rear
   10 Gas Tank
   11 Bed Sides (R & L)

|12| Fender (R & L) |15| Bear Bumper
|13| Rear Fender |16| Bed Bottom
|14| Spreader

9. On the table saw, saw to the appropriate thickness and cut the necessary angles on the following parts. See drawings for details.

|1| Cab Roof |12| Fender (R & L)
|3| Engine Hood |13| Rear Fender
|4| Tri Pod Top |14| Spreader
|5| Tri Pod Leg |15| Rear Bumper
|9| Bed Front & Rear |16| Bed Bottom
|11| Bed Sides (R & L)

10. Cut out the three wheels |6| and the axles |17| and |18| on the band saw. Allow a small amount of wood to remain beyond the pencil lines. Final shaping and smoothing will be done on the disc sander.

11. Drill axle holes into the following parts. See the drawings for details.

|5| Tri Pod Legs
|6| Wheels
|8| Base

12. Disc sand the wheels |6| to shape.

13. Belt sand all flat surfaces to remove scratches and blemishes, sanding with the grain of the wood.

14. Smooth all rough edges and corners.

Assembly

Note: For how to glue and dowel parts together, see the procedure described in the Introduction.

1. Glue and dowel the following parts together to form the truck bed.

|9| Bed Front and Rear
|11| Bed Sides (R & L)
|16| Bed Bottom

2. Glue and dowel the following parts together to form front wheel and axle housing section.

|4| Tri Pod Top |6| Front Wheel
|5| Tri Pod Legs (R & L) |17| Front Axle

3. Glue and dowel the following parts together to form the cab assembly.

|1| Cab Roof |3| Engine Hood
|2| Cab Post |7| Cab Sides

4. Glue and dowel the following parts together.

|8| Base
|10| Gas Tanks
|15| Bumper

5. Glue and dowel the remaining parts and sections together to form the Tri-Pod Truck.

6. Sand the surface of the truck to remove scratches and blemishes.

7. Apply one or two coats of boiled linseed oil.

Figure 23–2 Top and front views of Tri-Pod Truck.

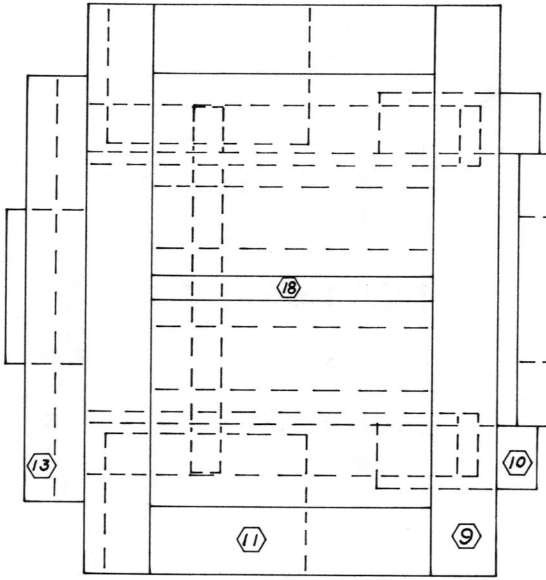

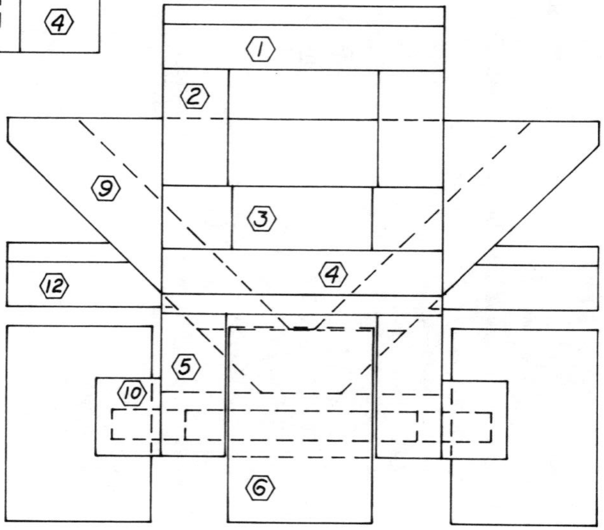

FRONT VIEW

TOP VIEW

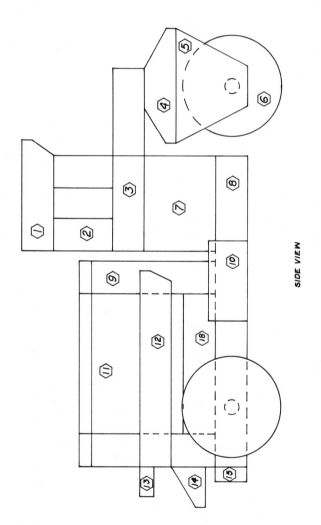

SIDE VIEW

Figure 23–3   Side view of Tri-Pod Truck.

151

Figure 23-4 Tri-Pod Truck patterns.

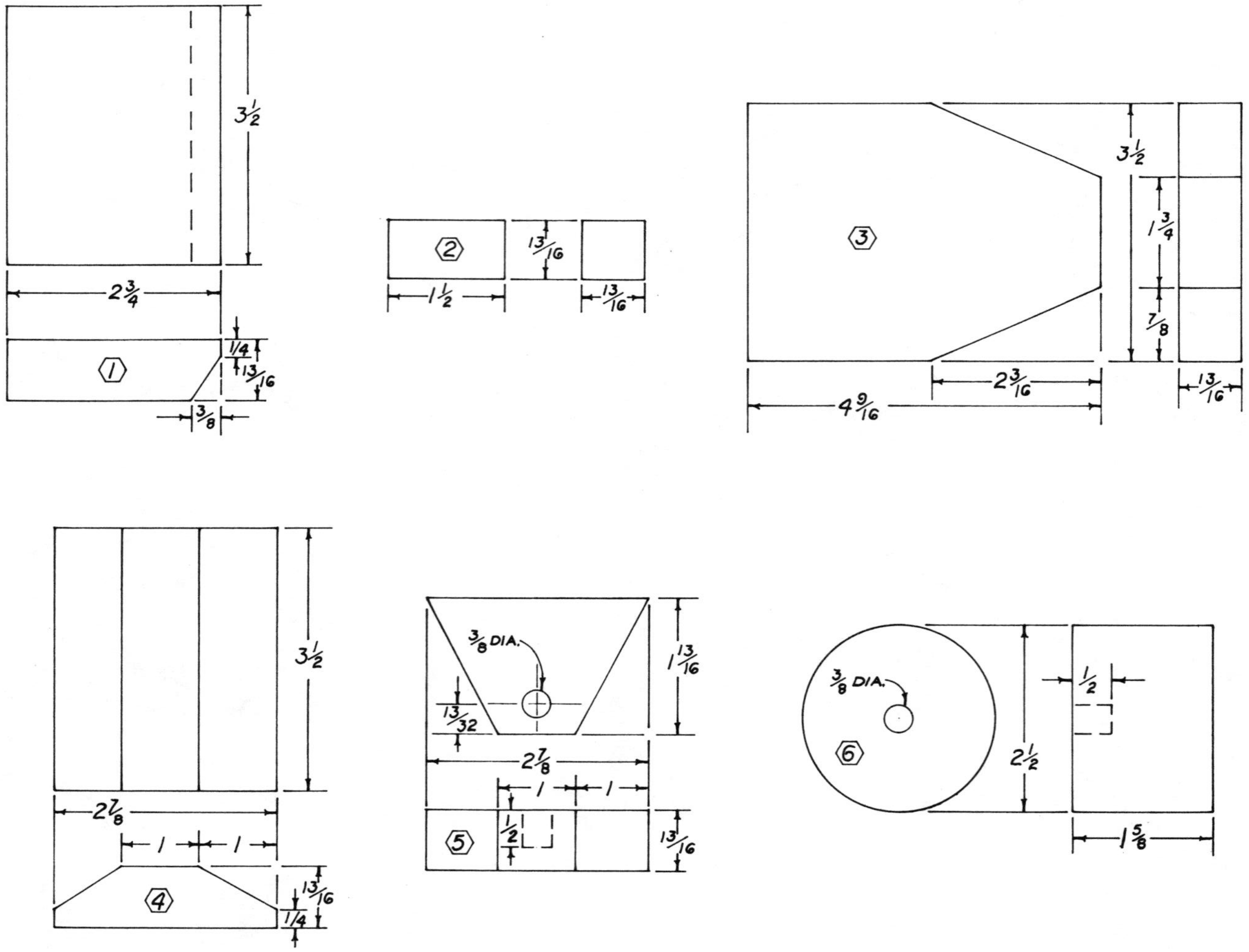

152

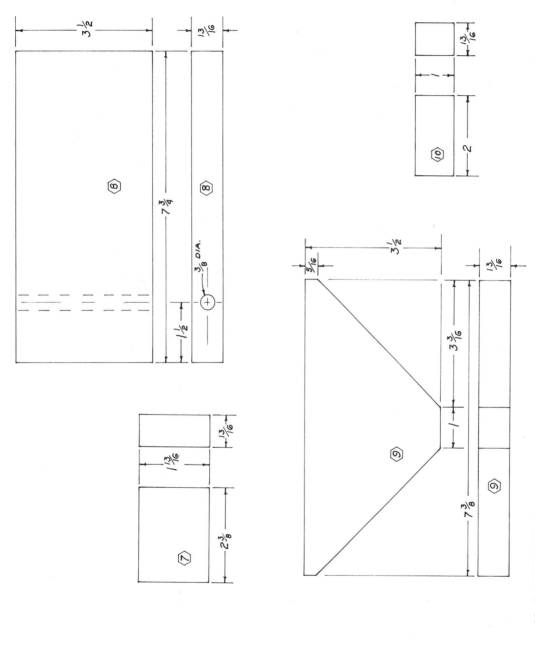

Figure 23–5   Tri-Pod Truck patterns.

153

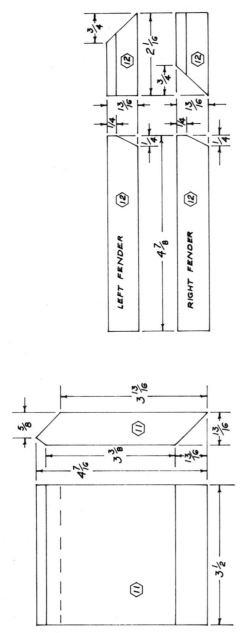

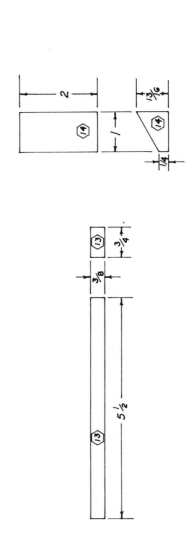

Figure 23-7 Tri-Pod Truck patterns.

154

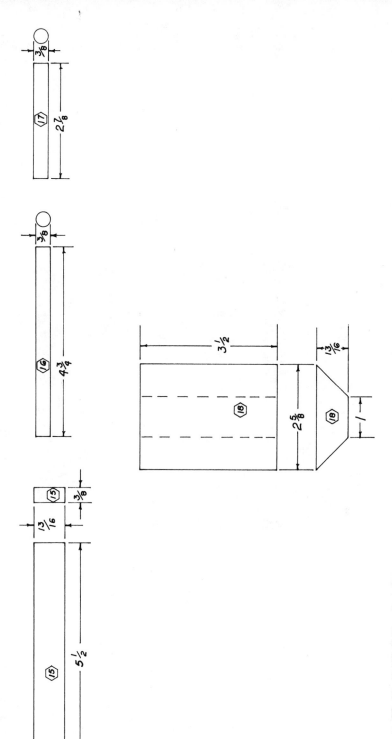

Figure 23–7 Tri-Pod Truck patterns.

155

·24·
Wood Wagon

Figure 24–1

The Wood Wagon has the appearance of "what used to be,"
before all of our products were mass-produced.
As the wagon is pulled, the axles squeak and tell mom that
junior is on the move.

PART	DIMENSIONS (thickness x width x length)	QUANTITY
1. Side	$\frac{13}{16}$ x 6 x 18	2
2. Front and Back	$\frac{13}{16}$ x 6 x 10	1 each
3. Wheel	$1\frac{5}{8}$ x 6 dia.	4
4. Front Axle Housing	$1\frac{5}{8}$ x 3 x 4	2
5. Rear Axle Housing	$1\frac{5}{8}$ x $3\frac{13}{16}$ x 4	2
6. Wagon Bottom	$\frac{13}{16}$ x $10\frac{3}{4}$ x 17	1
7. Handle	$\frac{13}{16}$ x $5\frac{1}{2}$ x 7	1
8. Handle Peg Nut	$\frac{13}{16}$ x $1\frac{1}{2}$ dia.	2
9. Tongue Peg Nut	$\frac{13}{16}$ x 2 dia.	2
10. Top Steering Axle Peg Nut	$\frac{13}{16}$ x 2 dia.	1
11. Tongue Hinge	$\frac{13}{16}$ x $1\frac{3}{4}$ x 3	2
12. Axle Washer	$\frac{13}{16}$ x 4 dia.	1
13. Axle Brace	$\frac{13}{16}$ x 4 x $11\frac{5}{8}$	2
14. Tongue Brace	$\frac{13}{16}$ x $1\frac{3}{4}$ x 8	2
15. Cross Tongue Brace	$\frac{13}{16}$ x $1\frac{3}{4}$ x $6\frac{1}{2}$	1
16. Tongue	$\frac{13}{16}$ x $1\frac{1}{4}$ x 21	1
17. Axle	$\frac{1}{2}$ dia. x 13	2
18. Bottom Steering Axle Peg Nut	$\frac{13}{16}$ x $2\frac{1}{2}$ dia.	1
19. Tongue Axles	$\frac{3}{8}$ dia. x $3\frac{3}{8}$	2
20. Main Steering Axle	$1\frac{1}{2}$ dia. x $4\frac{1}{2}$	1
21. Bottom Brace	$\frac{13}{16}$ x 4 x 10	2

Construction

1. Redraw the Wood Wagon patterns to full scale, using the dimensions shown in Figures 24–4 through 24–9.
2. Select the amount of clean, blemish-free hardwood stock needed to complete the Wood Wagon.
3. If not already milled, mill the rough 1″ woodstock to $\frac{13}{16}$″ thickness. Laminate $\frac{13}{16}$″ woodstock to desired thickness for the main steering axle. Use $\frac{13}{16}$″ woodstock for the wheels and front axle housing.
4. Prepare the production patterns as needed. Label each one for later use.
5. Place the milled woodstock on a worktable and draw or trace all of the Wood Wagon parts onto it.

6. Cut the hardwood into easy-to-handle lengths on the radial arm saw. Be careful not to cut through any toy parts during this process.

7. Joint the edges of the milled woodstock on the jointer. This provides a straight edge to guide future cuts on the table saw and radial arm saw.

8. On the table saw or radial arm saw, cut the following parts to the exact rectangular dimensions listed previously.

[1]	Sides	[11]	Tongue Hinge
[2]	Front and Back	[13]	Axle Brace
[4]	Front Axle Housing	[14]	Tongue Brace
[5]	Rear Axle Housing	[15]	Cross Tongue Brace
[6]	Wagon Bottom	[16]	Tongue
[7]	Handle	[21]	Bottom Brace

9. Make dado cuts into the following parts. See the drawings for details.

[1]	Sides	[14]	Tongue Brace
[2]	Front & Back	[15]	Cross Tongue Brace

10. Cut the following parts to size, shape, and length on the band saw. See the drawings for details.

[3]	Wheels	[10]	Top Steering Axle Peg Nut
[4]	Front Axle Housing (cut angles only)	[11]	Tongue Hinges
[5]	Rear Axle Housing (cut angles only)	[12]	Axle Washer
		[17]	Axle
[7]	Handle	[18]	Bottom Steering Axle Peg Nut
[8]	Handle Peg Nuts	[19]	Axle
[9]	Tongue Peg Nuts	[23]	Axle

When cutting on the band saw, allow a small amount of wood to remain outside the pencil lines. The final shaping will be done on the disc, belt, and drum sanders.

11. Shape the following parts on the disc sander and drum sander.

[3]	Wheels	[10]	Top Steering Axle Peg Nut
[7]	Handle	[11]	Tongue Hinges (top ends only)
[8]	Handle Peg Nuts	[12]	Axle Washer
[9]	Tongue Peg Nuts	[18]	Bottom Steering Axle Peg Nut

12. Drill axle holes, pivot holes, steering axle hole, etc. into the following parts on the drill press. See the drawings for details.

[3]	Wheels	[10]	Top steering Axle Peg Nut
[4]	Front Axle Housing	[11]	Tongue Hinge
[5]	Rear Axle Housing	[12]	Axle Washer
[6]	Wagon Bottom (main steering axle hole)	[13]	Axle Brace (front)
		[16]	Tongue
[7]	Handle (pivot hole and handle holes)	[17]	Axle
		[18]	Bottom Steering Axle Peg Nut
[8]	Handle Peg Nut	[19]	Axle
[9]	Tongue Peg Nut	[23]	Axle

Assembly

Note: For how to glue and dowel parts together, see the procedure described in the Introduction.

1. Glue and dowel the Wood Wagon together by sections: the wagon box, the axle sections, and the wagon tongue, etc. See the drawings for details.
2. Glue the wheels to the axles as the last step of assembly.
3. The dado cuts on the sides will be visible at each end of the wagon. Plug the cuts with square plugs.
4. Sand the surface of the Wood Wagon to remove scratches and blemishes. Sand with the grain to avoid scratching the wood.
5. Finish the surface with one or two coats of boiled linseed oil.

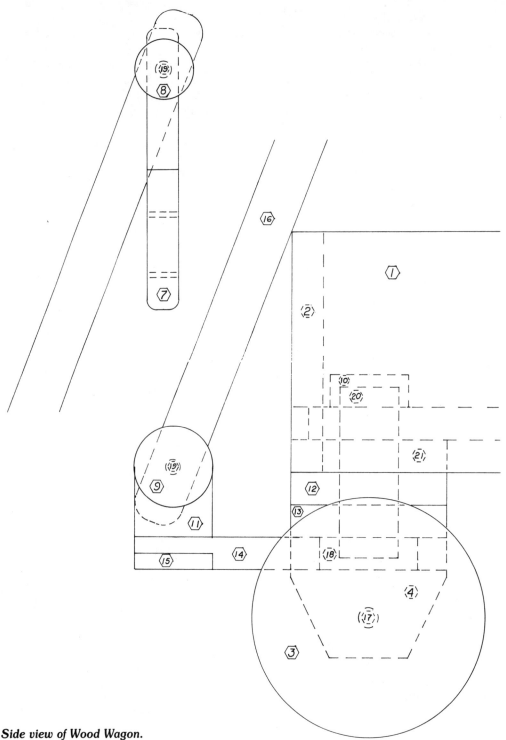

Figure 24–2   Side view of Wood Wagon.

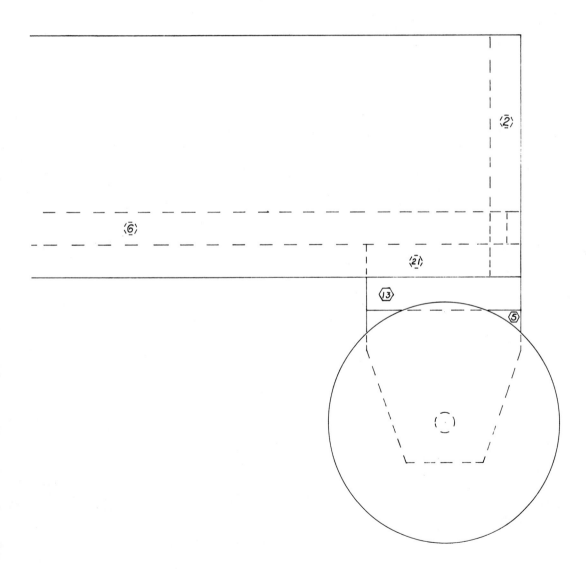

Figure 24–3 Front view of Wood Wagon.

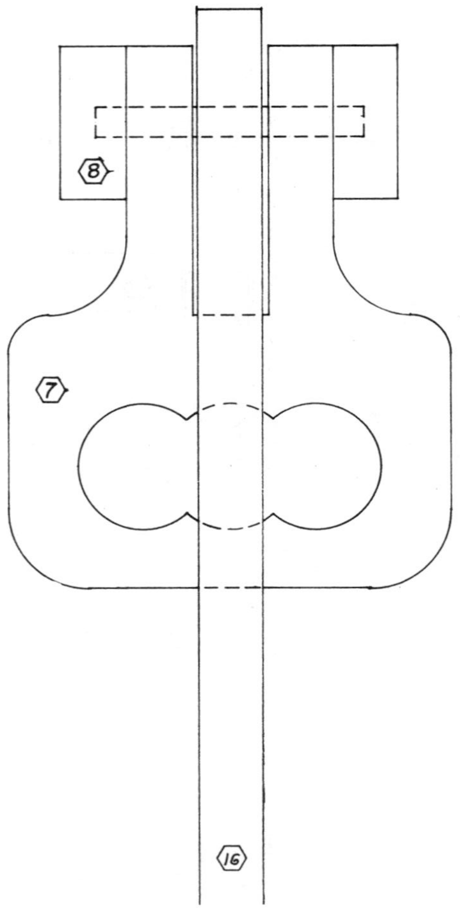

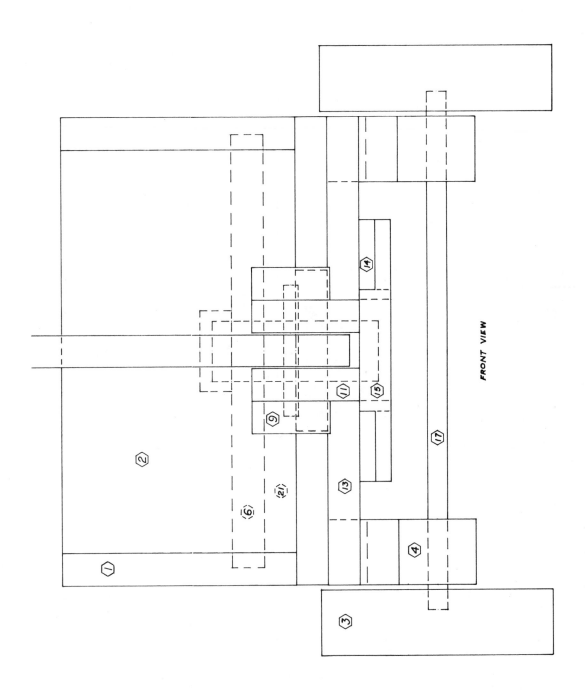

FRONT VIEW

163

Figure 24–4 Wood Wagon patterns.

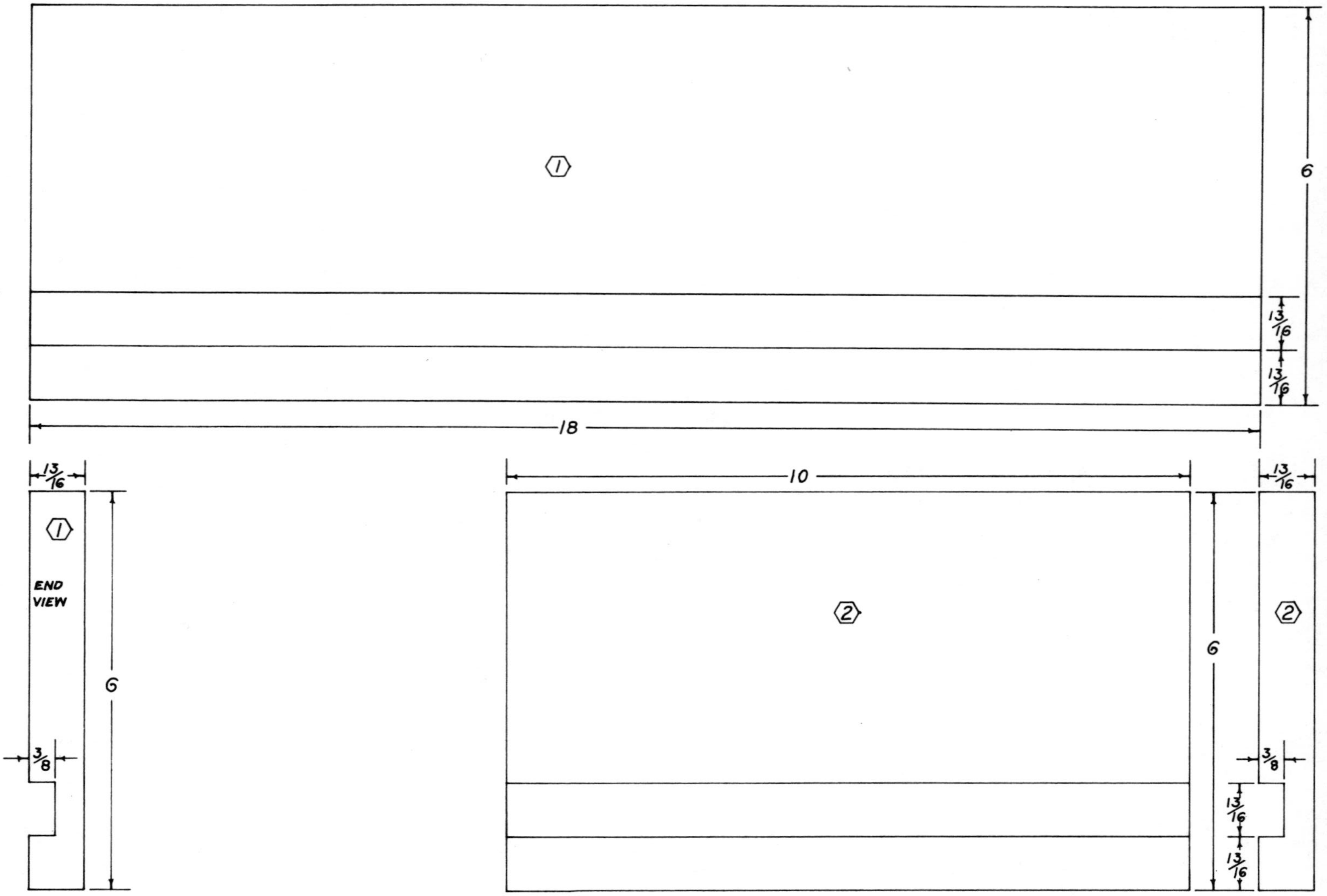

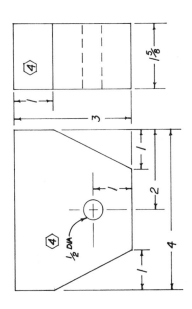

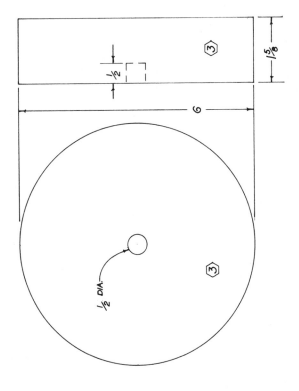

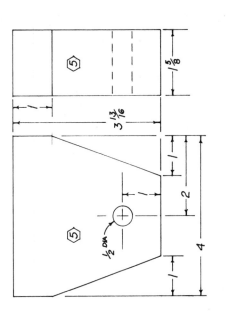

Figure 24–5 Wood Wagon patterns.

165

Figure 24-6 Wood Wagon patterns.

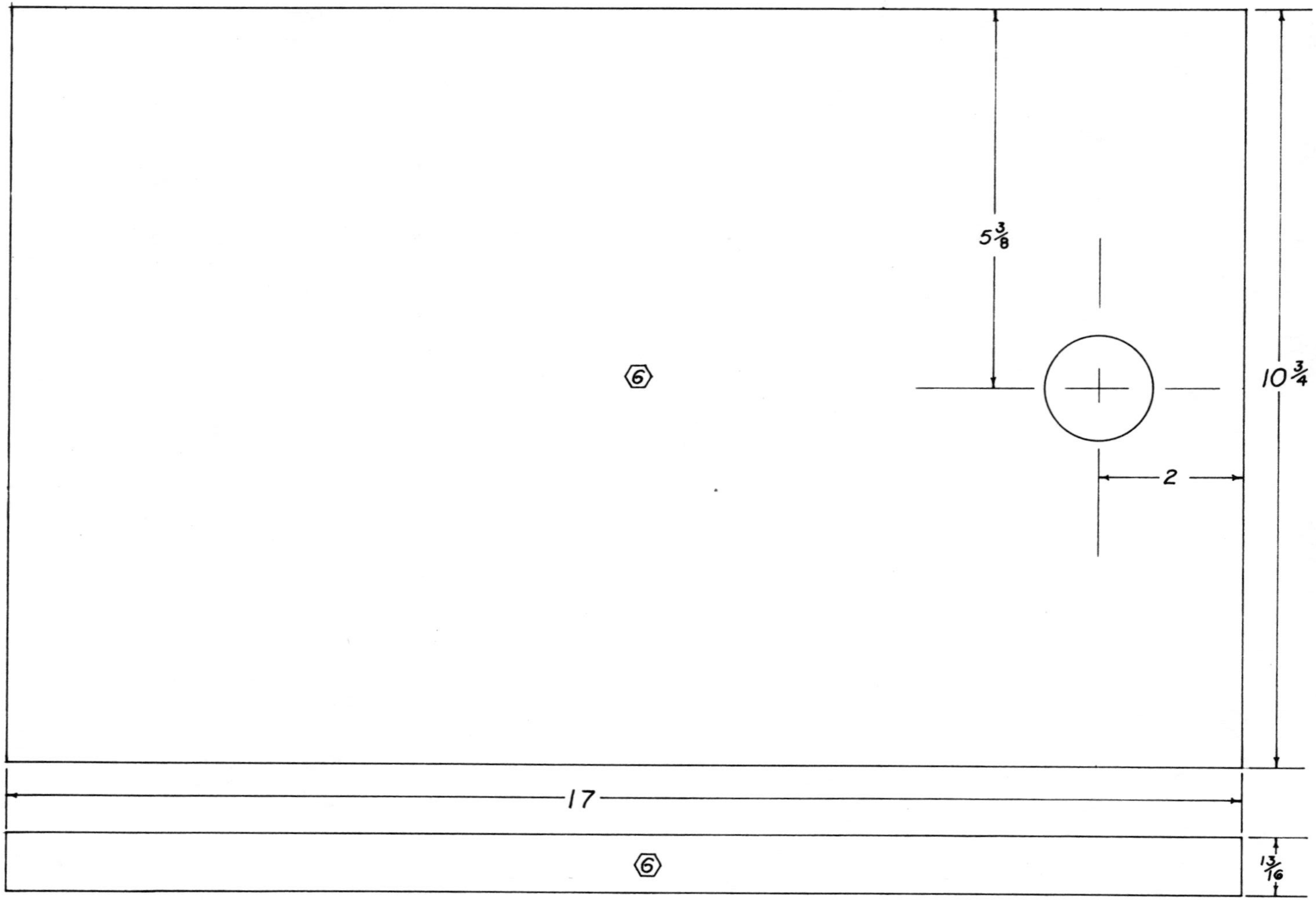

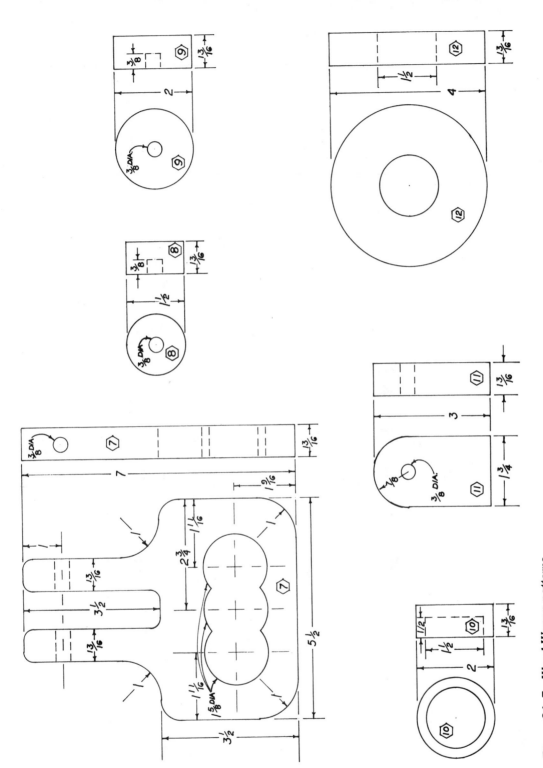

Figure 24-7   Wood Wagon patterns.

167

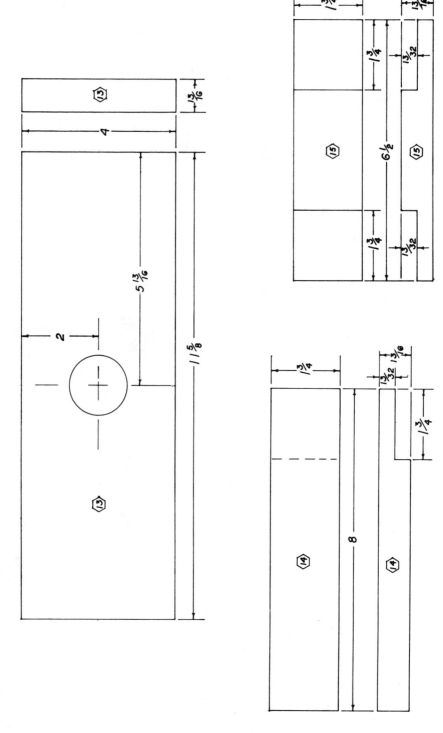

Figure 24-8 Wood Wagon patterns.

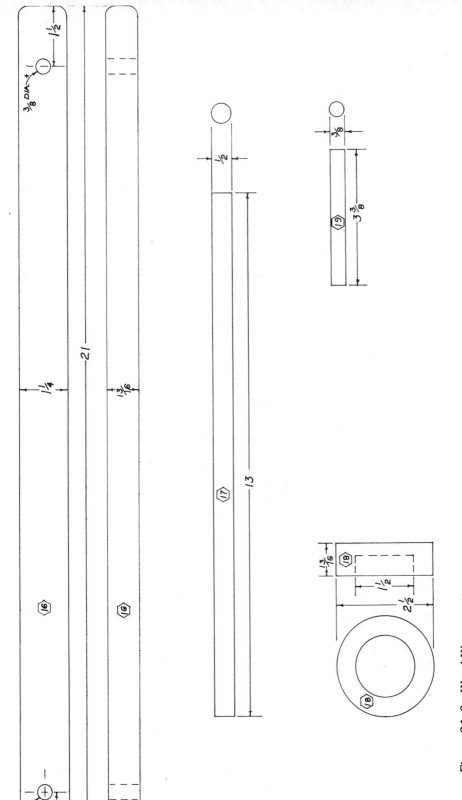

Figure 24–9 Wood Wagon patterns.

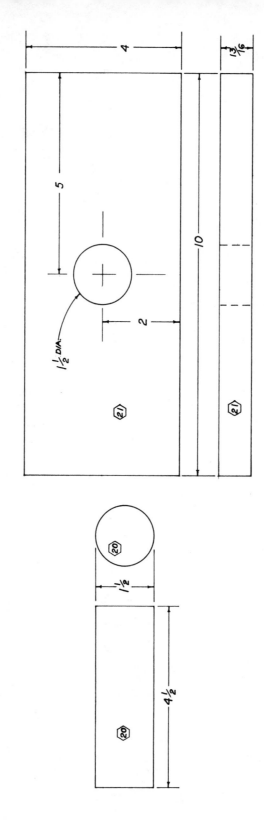

Figure 24–10 Wood Wagon patterns.

·25·
Bucket of Puzzles

Figure 25–1

The Bucket of Puzzles is a child's game testing speed and
manipulative skill. The procedure is to dump the six puzzles on
the rug, mix the pieces, and then see how long it takes the
person playing the game to put the puzzles back into the
bucket properly.

PART	DIMENSIONS (thickness x width x length)	QUANTITY
1. Top Ring	$\frac{13}{16}$ x $\frac{7}{8}$ x $9\frac{5}{8}$ dia.	1
2. Side Slat	$\frac{13}{16}$ x $1\frac{7}{8}$ x $7\frac{1}{4}$	16
3. Puzzle Ring	$\frac{13}{16}$ x $7\frac{3}{4}$ dia.	6
4. Bucket Bottom	$\frac{13}{16}$ x $8\frac{3}{4}$ dia.	1
5. Handles	$\frac{13}{16}$ x $1\frac{15}{16}$ dia.	2
6. Splines	$\frac{1}{8}$ x $\frac{3}{4}$ x $7\frac{1}{4}$	16

Construction

1. Redraw the Bucket of Puzzles patterns to full scale, using the dimensions shown in Figures 25–4 and 25–5.
2. Select the amount of clean, blemish-free hardwood needed to complete the Bucket of Puzzles.
3. If not already milled, mill the rough 1″ woodstock to $\frac{13}{16}$″ thickness.
4. Prepare the production patterns as needed. Label each pattern for later use.
5. Place the milled woodstock on a worktable and draw or trace all of the Bucket of Puzzle parts onto it.
6. Cut the hardwood into easy-to-handle lengths on the radial arm saw, being careful not to cut through any of the toy parts.
7. To get a flat edge to guide future cuts on the table saw and radial arm saw, joint the edges of the milled woodstock on the jointer.
8. Cut the side slats ② and splines ⑥ to exact rectangular dimensions on the table saw or radial arm saw. See drawings for details.
9. Cut the angles on the side slats ② as indicated on the drawings. Make the spline cuts in the side slats ② at this time also.
10. Place the dado head on the table saw or radial arm saw and cut the bottom groove into the side slats ②. This is the groove where the bucket bottom ④ is fitted during assembly.
11. Cut the following parts out on the band saw.

    ① Top Ring   ④ Bucket Bottom
    ③ Puzzle Rings   ⑤ Bucket Handles

    When cutting, allow a small amount of wood to remain beyond the pencil lines. Final shaping is done on the disc sander and drum sander.
12. Draw whatever designs you wish on the six puzzle boards. It is best to avoid sharp curves and corners. Long and smooth curves make for easier finish work on the disc, drum, and belt sanders.
13. Cut the puzzle designs on the band saw, using a fine tooth band saw blade. Follow your pencil lines exactly.
14. Disc, belt, and drum sand the edges of the puzzles to remove saw blade scratches. Do not over sand the edges.

15. Belt sand all of the flat surfaces to remove scratches and blemishes. Sand with the grain of the wood, not against it.

Assembly

1. Fit the bucket bottom 4 into the grooves in the side slats 2. Glue and spline (if desired) the side slats 2 as you build them around the bucket bottom 4. See drawings for spline details.
2. After the side slats 2 have been splined and glued together around the bucket bottom 4, place a strap clamp round the top and bottom part of the bucket and tighten to hold in place. Remove excess glue as the strap clamps are tightened.
3. Drill one $\frac{1}{4}$" dowel hole through each side slat 2 and into the bucket bottom 4. Place glue into the dowel holes, tap dowels into the holes and allow to dry.
4. Using bar clamps, clamp the top ring 1 into place around the top of the bucket. Drill one $\frac{1}{4}$" dowel hole for each side slat 2 from the top ring 1 through and into the side slats 2. Place a small amount of glue into the dowel holes. Tap one dowel into each dowel hole and then allow the bucket to dry.
5. Remove the dowel ends protruding from the top ring 1 and side slats 2 by belt sanding.
6. Glue and dowel the handles 5 to the side slats 2. See the drawings for details. If you wish, you can tie a piece of rope to the handles for carrying.
7. Sand the surface of the Bucket of Puzzles to remove scratches and blemishes.
8. Apply one or two coats of boiled linseed oil to the surface.

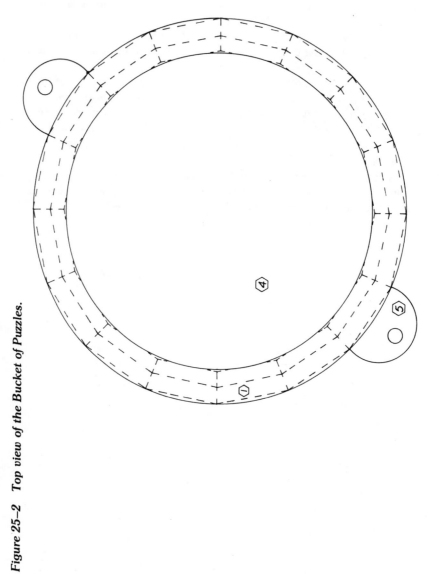

Figure 25–2 Top view of the Bucket of Puzzles.

TOP VIEW

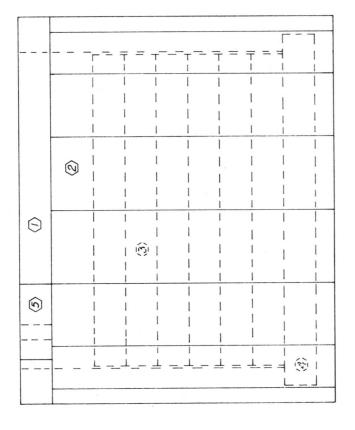

SIDE VIEW

Figure 25–3 Side view of the Bucket of Puzzles.

175

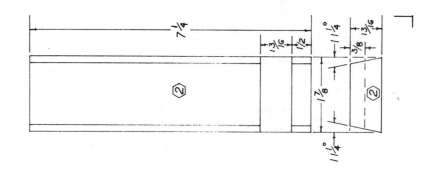

Figure 25–4 Bucket of Puzzles patterns.

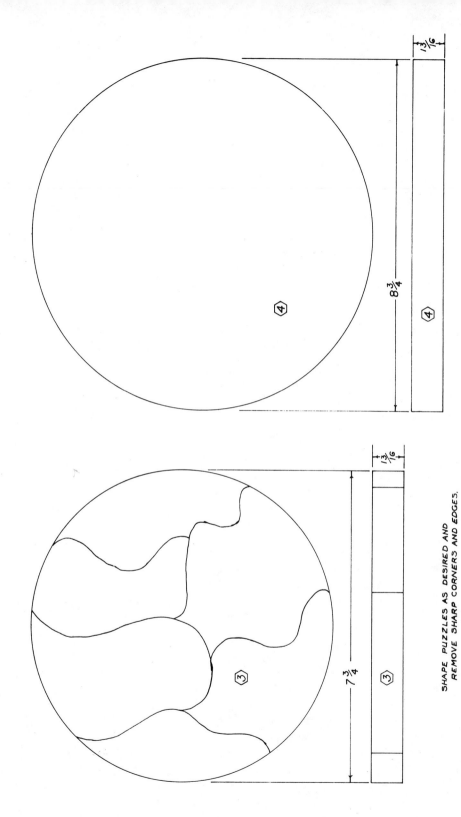

SHAPE PUZZLES AS DESIRED AND
REMOVE SHARP CORNERS AND EDGES.

Figure 25–5 Bucket of Puzzles patterns.

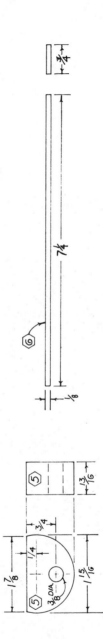

Figure 25–6 Bucket of Puzzles patterns.

·26·
Deno the Dino

Figure 26–1

In designing Deno the Dino, freehand sketching was used more than mechanical drawing tools. The offset cams that make the tail and head move are easy to design and can be adapted to the moving parts in other wooden toys.

PART	DIMENSIONS (thickness x width x length)	QUANTITY
1. Head and Neck	$\frac{13}{16}$ x $8\frac{3}{4}$ x $14\frac{5}{8}$	1
2. Body Side	$\frac{13}{16}$ x 7 x 10	2
3. Tail	$\frac{13}{16}$ x $7\frac{1}{8}$ x $12\frac{1}{2}$	1
4. Wheel	$1\frac{5}{8}$ x $5\frac{1}{2}$ dia.	4
5. Inner Brace	$\frac{13}{16}$ x 7 x $7\frac{1}{4}$	1
6. Cam Wheel	$\frac{13}{16}$ x $3\frac{5}{16}$ dia.	2
7. Axle	$\frac{1}{2}$ dia. x $3\frac{11}{16}$	2
8. Hinge Axle	$\frac{1}{2}$ dia. x $3\frac{11}{16}$	2
9. Eye Peg	$\frac{3}{8}$ dia. x $1\frac{11}{16}$	1
10. Peg Nut	$\frac{13}{16}$ x 1 dia.	6

Construction

1. Redraw the Deno the Dino patterns to full scale, using the dimensions shown in Figures 26–3 and 26–4.
2. Select the amount of clean, blemish-free hardwood stock needed to complete Deno The Dino.
3. If not already milled, mill the rough 1″ woodstock to $\frac{13}{16}$″ thickness. Laminate $\frac{13}{16}$″ woodstock to desired thickness for wheels or use 2″ woodstock.
4. Prepare the production patterns as needed. Label each one for later use.
5. Place the milled woodstock on a worktable and draw or trace all of Deno The Dino parts onto it.
6. For easier handling, cut the hardwood into pieces on the radial arm saw. Be sure not to cut through any of the toy parts.
7. Joint the edges of the milled woodstock on the jointer. This will give a straight edge to guide future cuts on the table saw and radial arm saw.
8. Cut the body sides ☐2 and inner brace ☐5 to the exact rectangular dimensions on the table saw or radial arm saw. See the drawings for details.
9. Cut the following parts to size and shape on the band saw.

☐1 Head and Neck	☐6 Cam Wheels
☐2 Body Sides (shape the corners)	☐7 Axles
☐3 Tail	☐8 Hinge Axles
☐4 Wheels	☐9 Eye Peg
☐5 Inner Brace (design as desired)	☐10 Peg Nuts

When cutting, allow a small amount of wood to remain beyond the pencil lines. Final shaping will be done on the disc, belt, and drum sanders.
10. Shape parts ☐1 through ☐10 on the disc, belt, and drum sanders.
11. Drill axle holes and hinge holes into the following parts. See the drawings for details.

☐1 Head and Neck (hinge and eye hole)	☐2 Body Sides (hinge and axle holes)

| 3 | Tail (hinge hole) | 6 | Cam Wheel (cam axle hole) |
| 4 | Wheel (axle hole) | 10 | Peg Nuts (peg holes) |

12. Belt sand all flat surfaces to remove scratches and blemishes. Be sure not to oversand.
13. Smooth all sharp edges and corners.

Assembly

Note: For how to glue and dowel parts together, see the procedure described in the Introduction.

1. Tap the axles 7 into the cam axle holes 6. Center the cam wheels 6 on the axles 7. Glue and dowel the cam wheel 6 to the axles 7 with $\frac{1}{4}$" dowel.
2. Insert the two axles 7 with the cam wheels 6 into the axle holes of the body sides 2. Then glue and dowel the body sides 2 and inner brace 5 together to form the main body of Deno The Dino.
3. Glue the wheels 4 to the axles 7.
4. Place the head and neck 1 and tail 3 into the spaces between the body sides 2. Insert the hinge axle 8 into the hinge holes and then glue the peg nuts 10 to each end of the hinge axles 8.
5. Place the eye peg 9 into the eye hole of the head 1 and then glue a peg nut 10 to each end of the eye peg 9.
6. Sand the surface of Deno The Dino to remove scratches and blemishes.
7. Apply one or two coats of boiled linseed oil.

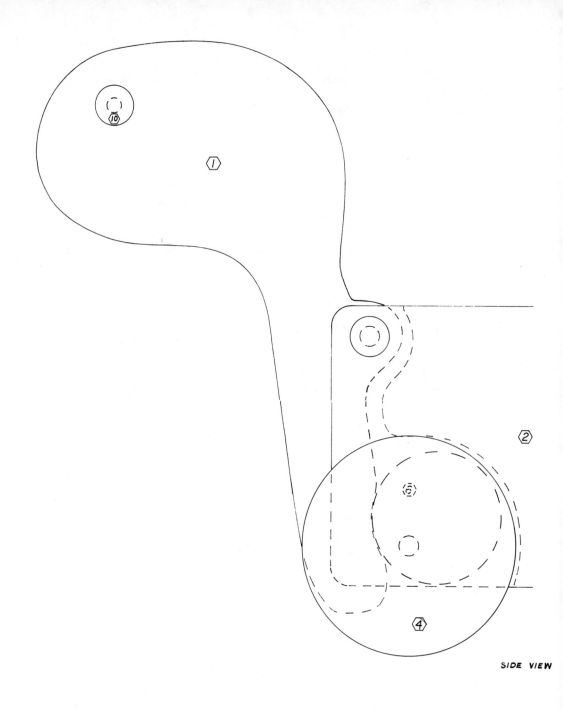

SIDE VIEW

Figure 26–2   Side view of Deno the Dino.

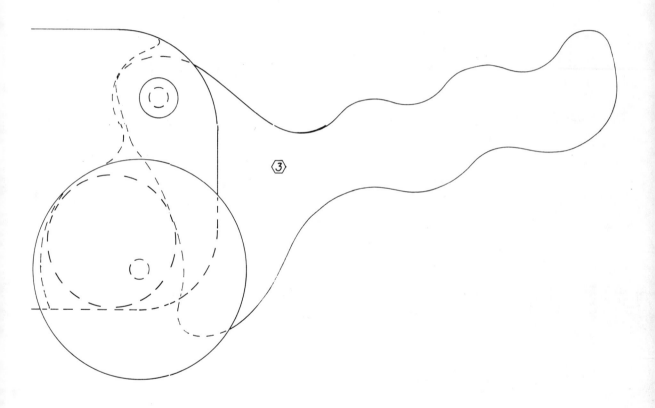

⟨3⟩

183

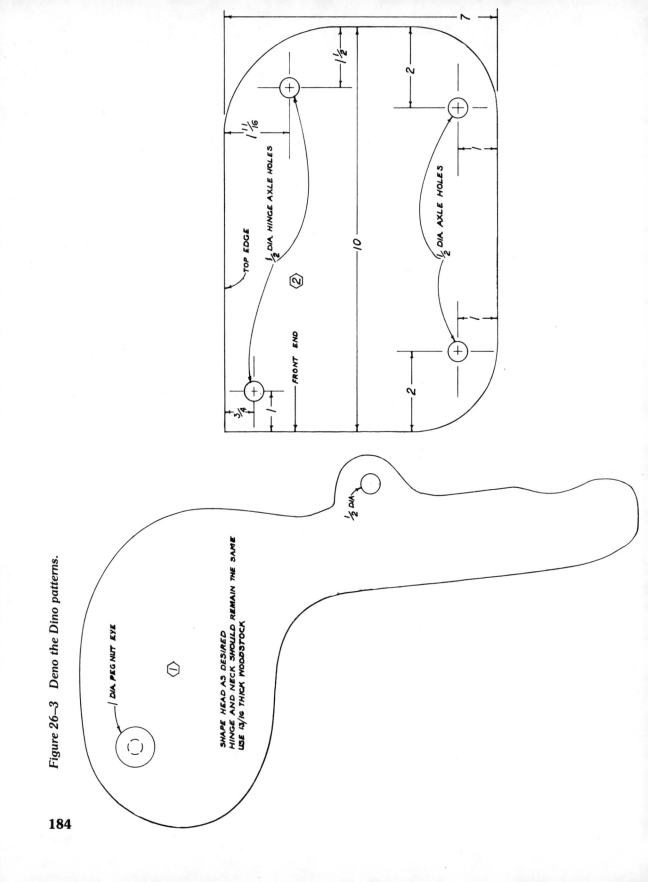

Figure 26–3 Deno the Dino patterns.

1 DIA. PEG NUT EYE

SHAPE HEAD AS DESIRED
HINGE AND NECK SHOULD REMAIN THE SAME
USE 13/16 THICK WOODSTOCK

½ DIA.

1

TOP EDGE

½ DIA HINGE AXLE HOLES

1 1/16

1½

7

2

½ DIA AXLE HOLES

FRONT END

10

2

3/4

1

2

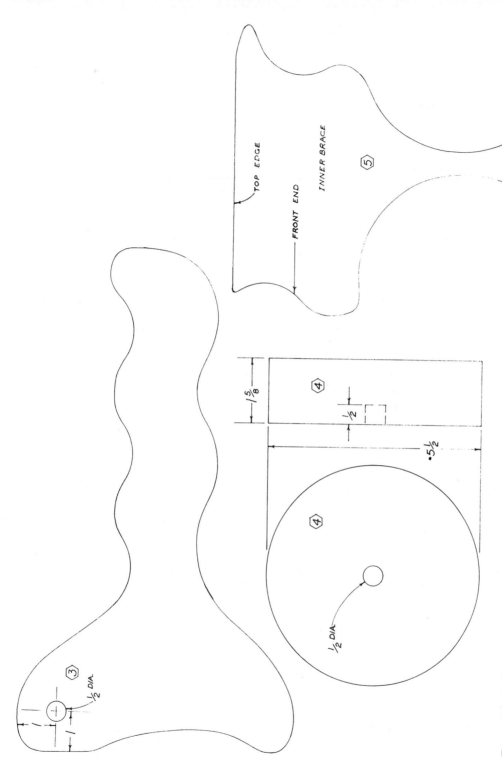

TOP EDGE

FRONT END

INNER BRACE

⑤

④

1 5/8

1/2

• 5 1/2

④

1/2 DIA

③

1/2 DIA.

1

Figure 26–4   Deno the Dino patterns.

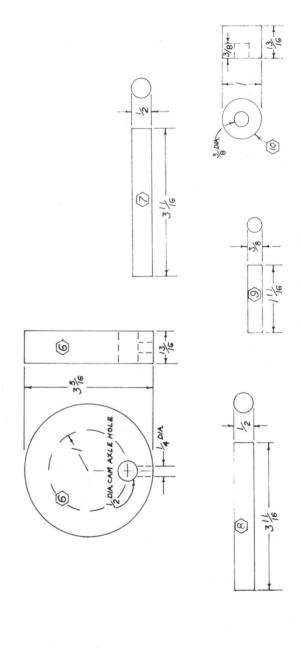

Figure 26–5   Deno the Dino patterns.

·27·
The Bug

Figure 27–1

Insects, or bugs, are fascinating to many children. The Bug can be fascinating, too, if you design it to create interest. The basic model illustrated here can be modified by changing the structure of the head and tail, or adding optional felt comb and tail to make The Bug move critter-like.

PART	DIMENSIONS (thickness x width x length)	QUANTITY
1. Inner Leg	$\frac{13}{16}$ x $\frac{3}{4}$ x $4\frac{1}{2}$	2
2. Wheel	$\frac{13}{16}$ x $2\frac{1}{4}$ dia.	4
3. Body	$\frac{13}{16}$ x $2\frac{1}{2}$ x 9	1
4. Axles	$\frac{3}{8}$ dia. x $1\frac{13}{16}$	2
5. Center Pivot Axle	$\frac{3}{8}$ dia. x $1\frac{13}{16}$	1
6. Leg Pivot Axle	$\frac{1}{4}$ dia. x $1\frac{1}{8}$	4
7. Outer Leg	$\frac{1}{2}$ x $\frac{3}{4}$ x $4\frac{1}{2}$	2
8. Peg Nut	$\frac{1}{2}$ dia. x $\frac{1}{2}$	4
9. Comb (red felt)	As desired	1
10. Tail (red or green felt)	As desired	1

Construction

1. Redraw The Bug patterns to full scale, using the dimensions shown in Figure 27–3.
2. Select the amount of clean, blemish-free hardwood stock needed to complete The Bug.
3. If not already milled, mill the rough 1″ woodstock to $\frac{13}{16}$″ thickness.
4. Prepare the production patterns as needed. Label each pattern for later use.
5. Place the milled woodstock on a worktable and draw or trace all of The Bug parts onto it.
6. For easier handling, cut the hardwood into pieces approximately 8″ long or longer on the radial arm saw.
7. For an even edge to guide future cuts on the table saw and radial arm saw, joint the edges of the milled woodstock on the jointer.
8. On the table saw or radial arm saw, cut the following parts to the exact rectangular dimensions listed previously.
   - ☐1 Inner Legs
   - ☐3 Body (also cut head and tail slots)
   - ☐7 Outer Legs
9. Cut the following parts to size and shape on the band saw. See the drawings for details.

☐2 Wheels	☐5 Center Pivot Axle
☐3 Body	☐6 Leg Pivot Axles
☐4 Axles	☐8 Peg Nuts

   When cutting on the band saw, allow a small amount of wood to remain outside the pencil lines. The final shaping will be done on the disc, belt, and drum sanders.
10. Shape the following parts on the disc sander and drum sander.

1. Inner Legs (round off each end)
2. Wheels
3. Body
4. Axles (taper ends slightly)
5. Center Axle Pivot (taper ends slightly)
6. Leg Axle Pivots (taper ends slightly)
7. Outer Legs (round off each end)
8. Peg Nuts

11. Drill holes into the following parts. See the drawings for details.
    1. Inner Legs
    2. Wheels
    3. Body
    7. Outer Legs
    8. Peg Nuts

12. Belt sand all flat surfaces to remove scratches and blemishes. Be careful not to oversand.
13. Smooth all rough edges and corners.

Assembly

1. Assemble The Bug by gluing and doweling the parts 1 through 10 together. Use any sequence that seems convenient.

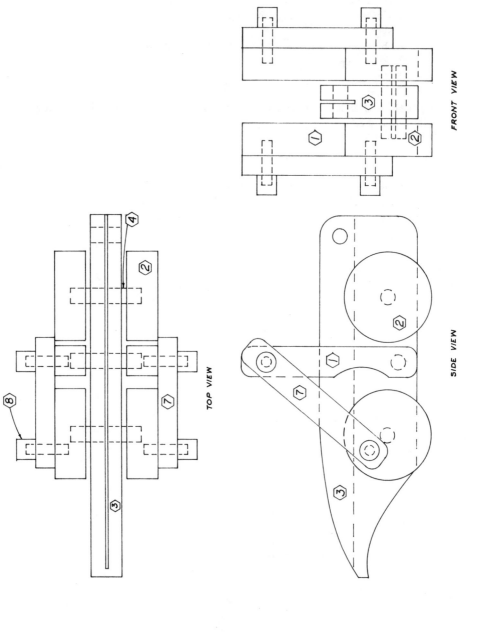

Figure 27–2   Top, side, and front views of The Bug.

FRONT VIEW

SIDE VIEW

TOP VIEW

190

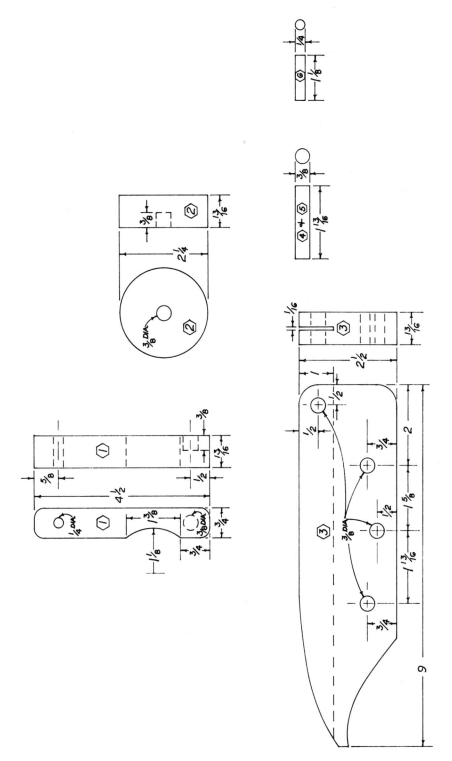

Figure 27-3 The Bug patterns.

191

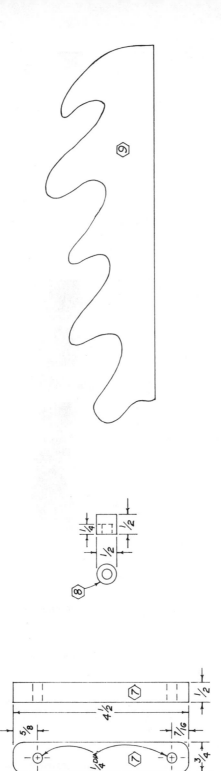

Figure 27–4 The Bug patterns.

· 28 ·
Antique Car

Figure 28–1

The Antique Car is a combination of many designs of the past.
It resembles in part a model T, an old pick-up truck,
or one of the very early sports cars. Children will enjoy its
interesting design.

PART	DIMENSIONS (thickness x width x length)	QUANTITY
1. Seat	2 x 4 x 4	1
2. Bed Side	$\frac{13}{16}$ x 2 x $7\frac{3}{4}$	2
3. Base	$\frac{13}{16}$ x 4 x $12\frac{1}{4}$	1
4. Fire Wall	$\frac{1}{2}$ x 3 x 4	1
5. Engine	2 x 4 x 4	1
6. Front Fender	$\frac{13}{16}$ x $3\frac{1}{4}$ x $4\frac{1}{4}$	2
7. Spring	$\frac{13}{16}$ x 2 x $4\frac{1}{2}$	4
8. Wheel	$\frac{13}{16}$ x $3\frac{1}{2}$ dia.	4
9. Head Lamps	$\frac{1}{2}$ dia. x 1	2
10. Steering Wheel	$\frac{13}{16}$ x $1\frac{7}{8}$ dia.	1
11. Steering Post	$\frac{3}{8}$ dia. x $4\frac{3}{4}$	1
12. Rear Fender	$\frac{13}{16}$ x 2 x $6\frac{1}{2}$	2 (R & L)
13. Tail Gate	$\frac{13}{16}$ x 2 x $2\frac{3}{8}$	1
14. Axle	$\frac{3}{8}$ dia. x 5	2

Construction

1. Redraw the Antique Car patterns to full scale, using the dimensions shown in Figures 28–5, 28–6 and 28–7.
2. Select the amount of clean, blemish-free hardwood stock needed to complete the Antique Car.
3. If not already milled, mill the rough 1″ woodstock to $\frac{13}{16}$″ thickness.
4. Laminate enough $\frac{13}{16}$″ woodstock to form the desired thickness for the seat [1] and engine [5]. Glue and clamp the wood together and allow to dry.
5. Prepare and label the production patterns as needed.
6. Place the milled woodstock on a worktable and draw or trace all of the Antique Car parts onto it.
7. Cut the hardwood into easy-to-handle lengths on the radial arm saw. Be sure not to cut through any of the car parts in the process.
8. Joint the edges of the milled woodstock on the jointer. This gives a straight edge to guide future cuts on the table saw and radial arm saw.
9. On the table saw or radial arm saw, cut the following parts to the exact rectangular dimensions listed previously.

   [1] Seat
   [2] Bed Sides
   [3] Base
   [4] Fire Wall
   [5] Engine
   [6] Front Fender
   [7] Spring
   [12] Rear Fender
   [13] Tail Gate

10. Cut the following parts out on the band saw.

    [2] Bed Sides (cut out the front angle)
    [5] Engine (cut the rounded top)
    [6] Front Fenders

7	Springs	12	Rear Fenders
8	Wheels	14	Axles
10	Steering Wheel		

When cutting, allow a small amount of wood to remain beyond the pencil lines. Final shaping is done on the disc sander.

11. Shape the following parts on the disc, drum, and belt sanders.

2	Bed Sides (drum sand the front angle)	7	Springs (1″ belt sand)
5	Engine (disc sand the rounded top)	8	Wheels (disc sand)
6	Front Fender (disc and drum sand)	10	Steering Wheel
		12	Rear Fenders
		14	Axles (taper ends slightly)

12. Drill the correct size holes into the following parts. See the drawings for details.

3	Base	8	Wheels
7	Springs	10	Steering Wheel

13. Belt sand all of the flat surfaces to remove scratches and blemishes. Sand with the grain to avoid marring the wood.
14. Smooth all rough edges and corners.

Assembly

Note: For how to glue and dowel parts together, see the procedure described in the Introduction.

1. Glue and dowel the following parts together. See the drawings for details.

2	Bed Sides	5	Engine
3	Base	7	Springs
4	Fire Wall	13	Tail Gate

2. Glue and dowel the remaining parts together to form the body of the car. See the drawings for details.

1	Seat	10	Steering Wheel
6	Front Fenders	11	Steering Post
9	Head Lamps	12	Rear Fenders

3. Place the axles 14 into the axle holes in the springs 7 and then glue the wheels 8 to the axles 14.
4. Sand the surface of the Antique Car to remove scratches and blemishes.
5. Apply one or two coats of boiled linseed oil.

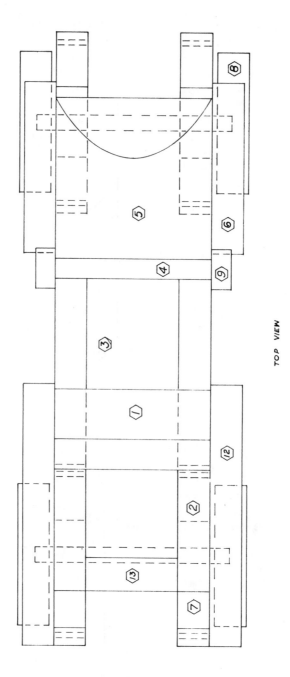

TOP VIEW

Figure 28–2 Top view of Antique Car.

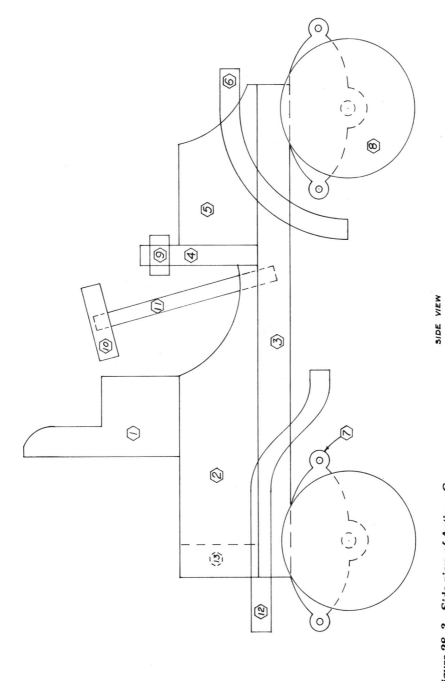

SIDE VIEW

Figure 28–3   Side view of Antique Car.

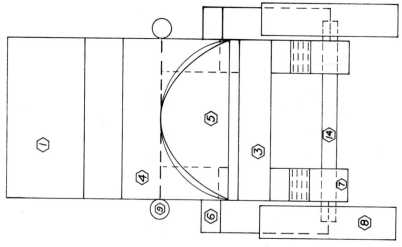

Figure 28–4 Front view of Antique Car.

FRONT VIEW

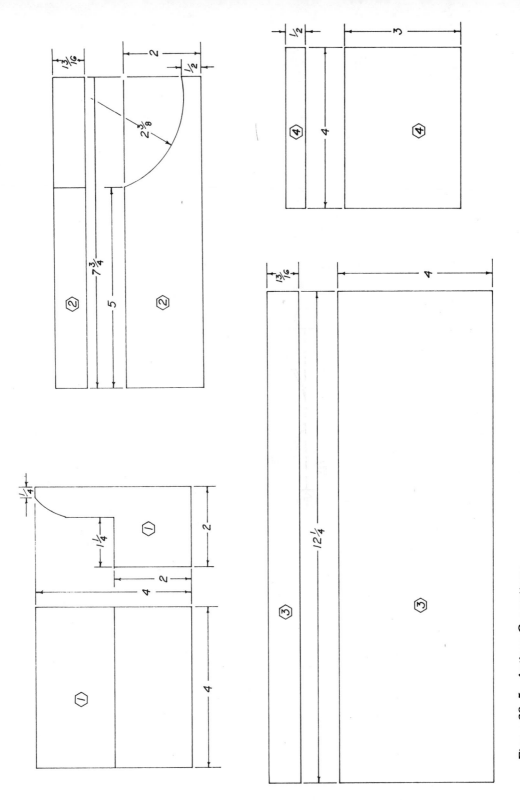

Figure 28–5 Antique Car patterns.

199

Figure 28-6 Antique Car patterns.

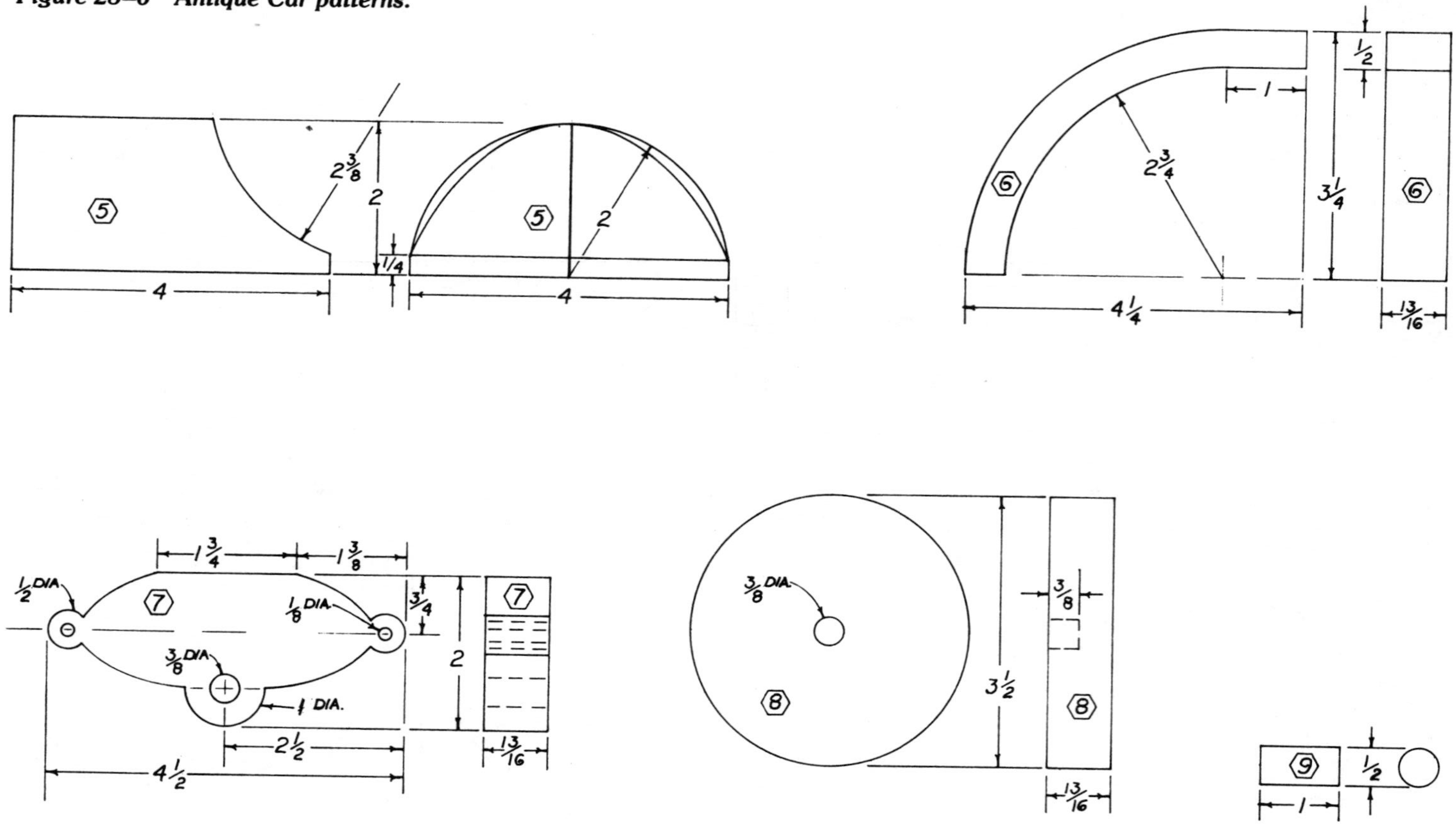

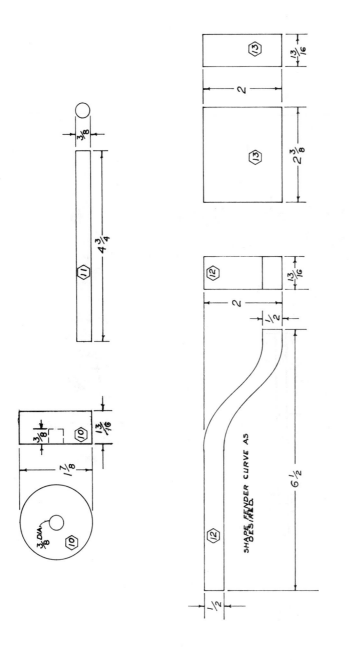

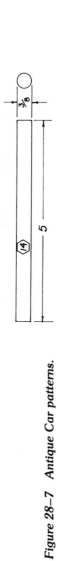

Figure 28–7   Antique Car patterns.

·29·
Delivery Truck

Figure 29–1

The Delivery Truck, or general utility truck, is needed for important business areas found behind chairs, sofas, and other furniture. Small blocks and odds and ends fit perfectly in the back of the truck.

PART	DIMENSIONS (thickness x width x length)	QUANTITY
1. Cab top	$\frac{13}{16}$ x 3 x $5\frac{5}{8}$	1
2. Cab Side	$\frac{13}{16}$ x $3\frac{11}{16}$ x $4\frac{1}{2}$	2
3. Grill	$\frac{13}{16}$ x $3\frac{5}{16}$ x $5\frac{5}{8}$	1
4. Wheel	$\frac{13}{16}$ x 2 dia.	4
5. Van Top	$\frac{13}{16}$ x $5\frac{5}{8}$ x $5\frac{3}{4}$	1
6. Van Side	$\frac{13}{16}$ x $5\frac{3}{4}$ x $5\frac{5}{8}$	2
7. Base	$\frac{13}{16}$ x 4 x $9\frac{11}{16}$	1
8. Van Front	$\frac{13}{16}$ x 4 x $4\frac{13}{16}$	1
9. Axle	$\frac{3}{8}$ dia. x 5	2

Construction

1. Redraw the Delivery Truck patterns to full scale, using the dimensions shown in Figures 29–3 and 29–4.
2. Select the amount of clean, blemish-free hardwood stock needed to complete the Delivery Truck.
3. If not already milled, mill the rough 1″ woodstock to $\frac{13}{16}$″ thickness.
4. Prepare the production patterns as needed. Label each pattern for later use.
5. Place the milled woodstock on a worktable and draw or trace all of the Delivery Truck parts onto it.
6. Cut the hardwood into easy-to-handle lengths on the radial arm saw. Be sure not to cut through any toy parts.
7. Joint the edges of the milled woodstock on the jointer. This provides a straight edge to guide future cuts on the table saw and radial arm saw.
8. On the table saw or radial arm saw, cut the following parts to the exact rectangular dimensions listed previously.
   - 1 Cab Top (also make slant cut)
   - 2 Cab Sides (also make slant cut)
   - 3 Grill (also make slant cut)
   - 5 Van Top
   - 6 Van Sides
   - 7 Base
   - 8 Van Front
9. Cut the wheels 4 to size and shape on the band saw.
10. Drill axle holes, window holes, and fender wells into the following parts. Use a circle saw for the windows and fender wells. See the drawings for details.
    - 2 Cab Sides
    - 4 Wheels
    - 6 Van Side
    - 7 Base
11. Disc sand the wheels 4 to size and shape.
12. Belt sand all of the flat surfaces to remove scratches and blemishes. Always sand with the grain of the wood.
13. Smooth all sharp edges and corners.

Assembly

Note: For how to glue and dowel parts together, see the procedure described in the Introduction.

1. Glue and dowel the following parts together to form the cab and body of the Delivery Truck. See the drawings for details.

    [1] Cab Top   [3] Grill

    [2] Cab Sides   [7] Base

2. Glue and dowel the following parts to the base [7] to form the van section. See the drawings for details.

    [5] Van Top

    [6] Van Sides

    [8] Van Front

3. Place the axles [9] into the axle holes of the base [7] and then glue the wheels [4] to the axles [9].

4. Sand all surfaces of the Delivery Truck.

5. Apply one or two coats of boiled linseed oil to the surface of the truck.

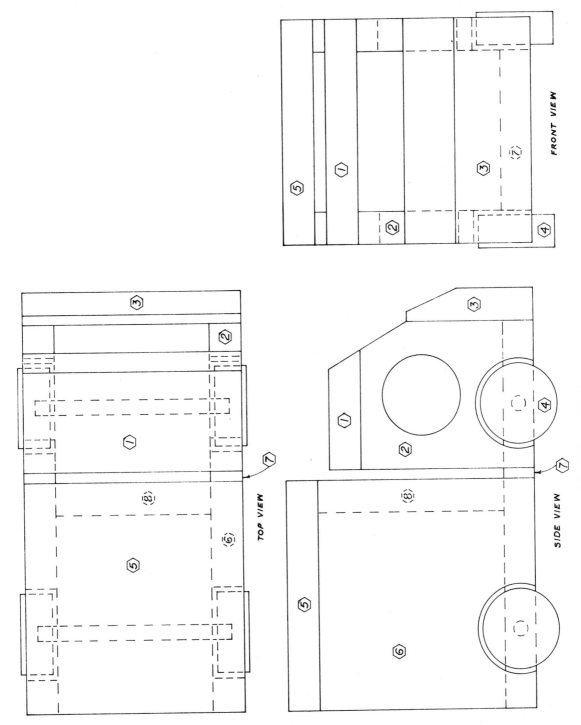

FRONT VIEW

TOP VIEW

SIDE VIEW

Figure 29–2 Top, side, and front views of the Delivery Truck.

Figure 29-3 Delivery Truck patterns.

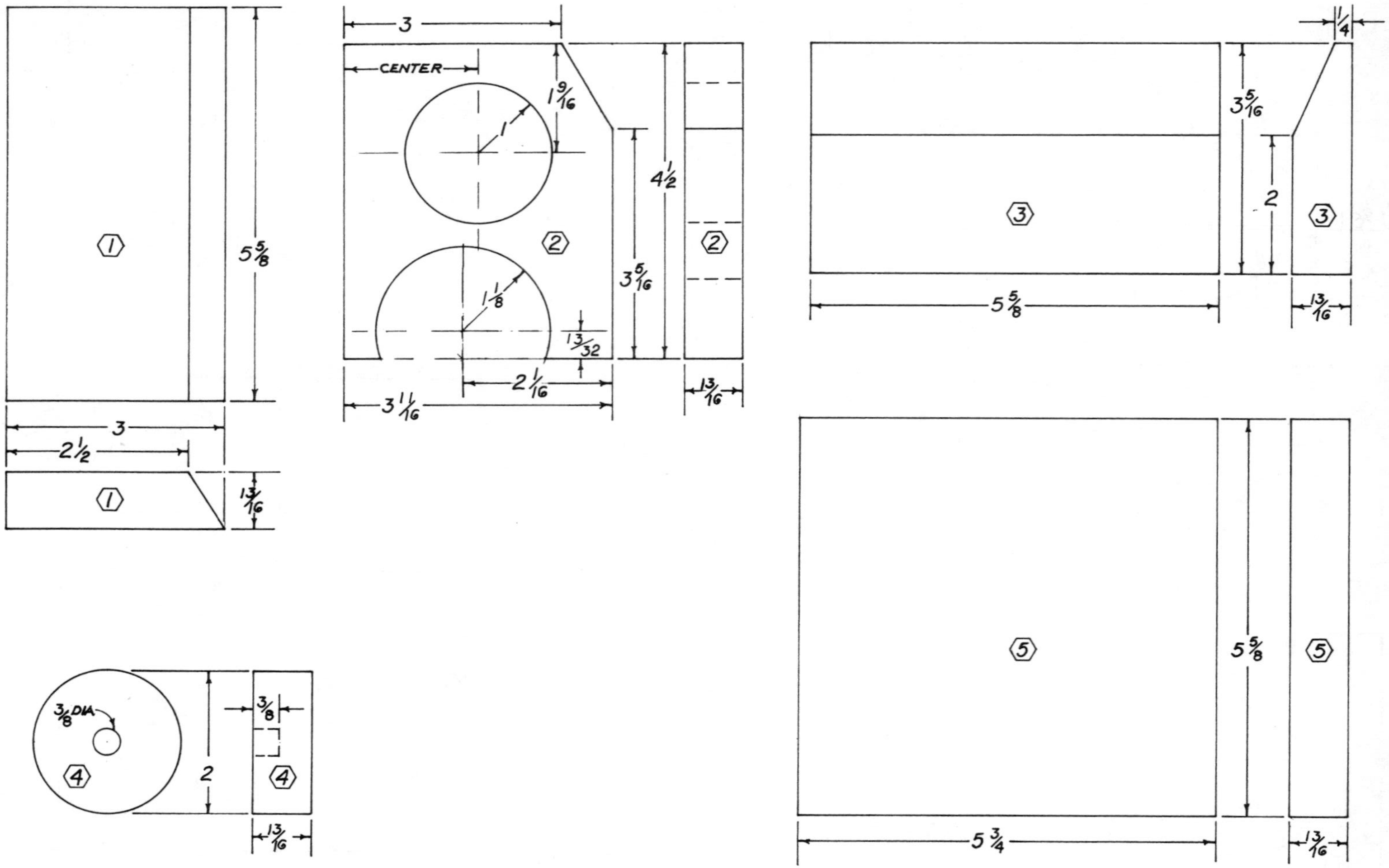

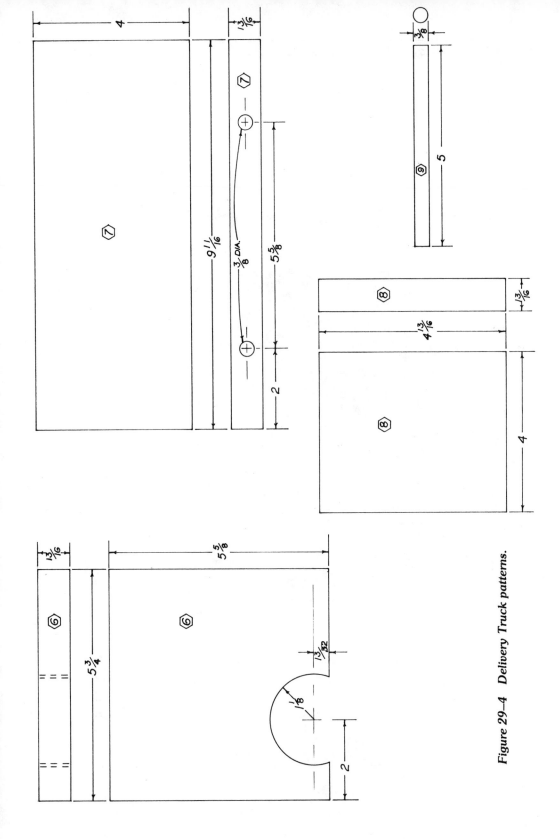

Figure 29-4 Delivery Truck patterns.

207

·30·
Dump Truck

Figure 30–1

Every child seems to love a dump truck. This one is fun to
play with and to build.

PART	DIMENSIONS (thickness x width x length)	QUANTITY
1. Cab Roof	$\frac{13}{16}$ x $3\frac{1}{2}$ x 4	1
2. Cab Side	$\frac{13}{16}$ x $2\frac{11}{16}$ x 5	2
3. Cab Front	$\frac{13}{16}$ x 4 x 5	1
4. Cab Floor	$\frac{13}{16}$ x 4 x $5\frac{1}{8}$	1
5. Base	$\frac{13}{16}$ x 4 x $9\frac{1}{2}$	1
6. Front Wheel	$1\frac{5}{8}$ x $2\frac{3}{8}$ dia.	2
7. Bed Side	$\frac{13}{16}$ x $4\frac{13}{16}$ x 8	2
8. Bed Bumper	$\frac{13}{16}$ x $2\frac{3}{16}$ x $7\frac{9}{16}$	2
9. Rear Wheel	$1\frac{5}{8}$ x 4 dia.	2
10. Bed Rail	$\frac{1}{2}$ x $2\frac{1}{4}$ x 6	1
11. Front Axle Housing	$\frac{13}{16}$ x 3 x 4	1
12. Bed Hinge	1 x $1\frac{1}{2}$ x $2\frac{1}{4}$	1
13. Bed Front	$\frac{13}{16}$ x $1\frac{7}{8}$ x $5\frac{7}{8}$	1
14. Bed Rear	$\frac{13}{16}$ x $1\frac{7}{8}$ x $5\frac{7}{8}$	1
15. Bed Bottom	$\frac{13}{16}$ x $5\frac{7}{8}$ x $7\frac{5}{8}$	1
16. Front Axle	$\frac{3}{8}$ dia. x 5	1
17. Rear Axle	$\frac{3}{8}$ dia. x 5	1
18. Hinge Axle Shaft	$\frac{3}{8}$ dia. x 4	1

Construction

1. Redraw the Dump Truck patterns to full scale, using the dimensions shown in Figures 30–5, 30–6, and 30–7.
2. Select the amount of clean, blemish-free hardwood stock needed to complete the Dump Truck.
3. If not already milled, mill the rough 1″ woodstock to $\frac{13}{16}$″ thickness.
4. Prepare the production patterns as needed. Label each pattern for later use.
5. Place the milled woodstock on a worktable and draw or trace all of the truck parts onto it.
6. Cut the hardwood into easy-to-handle lengths on the radial arm saw.
7. Joint the edges of the milled woodstock on the jointer. This provides a straight edge to guide future cuts on the table saw and radial arm saw.
8. On the table saw or radial arm saw, cut the following parts to the exact rectangular dimensions listed previously.

   1. Cab Roof (also cut slant)
   2. Cab Sides
   3. Cab Front
   4. Cab Floor
   5. Base
   7. Bed Side (also cut rear slant)
   8. Bed Bumper (also cut slants)
   10. Bed Rail (also saw to $\frac{1}{2}$″ thickness)
   11. Front Axle Housing (also cut slants)
   12. Bed Hinge (also cut slant)

13 Bed Front

14 Bed Rear (also cut angle as desired)

15 Bed Bottom (also cut slant)

9. Make dado cuts into the following parts. See the drawings for details.

4 Cab Floor

15 Bed Bottom

10. Cut the following parts to size and shape on the band saw. See the drawings for details.

6 Front Wheels   16 Front Axle

7 Bed Sides   17 Rear Axle

8 Bed Bumper   18 Hinge Axle Shaft

9 Rear Wheel

When cutting on the band saw, allow a small amount of wood to remain outside the pencil lines. The final shaping will be done on the disc, belt, and drum sanders.

11. Disc and belt sand the following parts to final size and shape. See the drawings for details.

6 Front Wheels   16 Front Axle (taper ends slightly)

7 Bed Sides (top curve only)   17 Rear Axle (taper ends slightly)

8 Bed Bumper   18 Hinge Axle Shaft (taper ends

9 Rear Wheel   slightly)

12. Drill holes into the following parts. See the drawings for details.

5 Base (axle hole)   9 Rear Wheel (axle hole)

6 Front Wheel (axle hole)   11 Front Axle Housing (axle hole)

8 Bed Bumper (hinge axle shaft   12 Bed Hinge (hinge axle shaft
   hole)   hole)

13. Remove all sharp edges and corners.

14. Belt sand all of the flat surfaces to remove scratches and blemishes.

Assembly

Note: For how to glue and dowel parts together, see the procedure described in the Introduction.

1. Glue and dowel the following parts together to form the cab.

1 Cab Roof   3 Cab Front

2 Cab Sides   4 Cab Floor

2. Glue and dowel the following parts together to form the dump bed.

7 Bed Sides   14 Bed Rear

8 Bed Bumper   15 Bed Bottom

13 Bed Front

3. Glue and dowel the following parts together to form the base.

5 Base   11 Front Axle Housing

10 Bed Rail   12 Bed Hinge

4. Glue and dowel the cab, dump bed, and base together to form the Dump Truck.

5. Place the hinge axle shaft ⌷18⌷ into the axle shaft holes of the bed bumper ⌷8⌷ and bed hinge. Glue the shaft to the bed bumper ⌷8⌷.

6. Place the front axle ⌷16⌷ and rear axle ⌷17⌷ into the axle holes and then glue the front wheels ⌷6⌷ to the front axle ⌷16⌷ and the rear wheels ⌷9⌷ to the rear axle ⌷17⌷.

7. Sand the Dump Truck to remove all scratches and blemishes.

8. To finish the surface, apply one or two coats of boiled linseed oil.

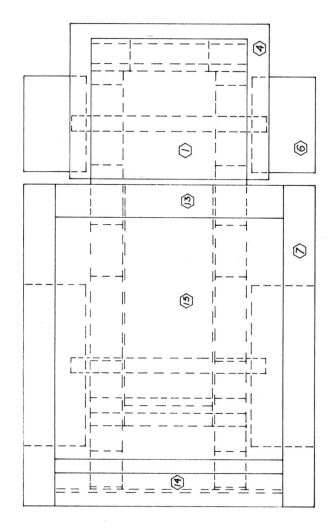

Figure 30–2 Top view of Dump Truck.

TOP VIEW

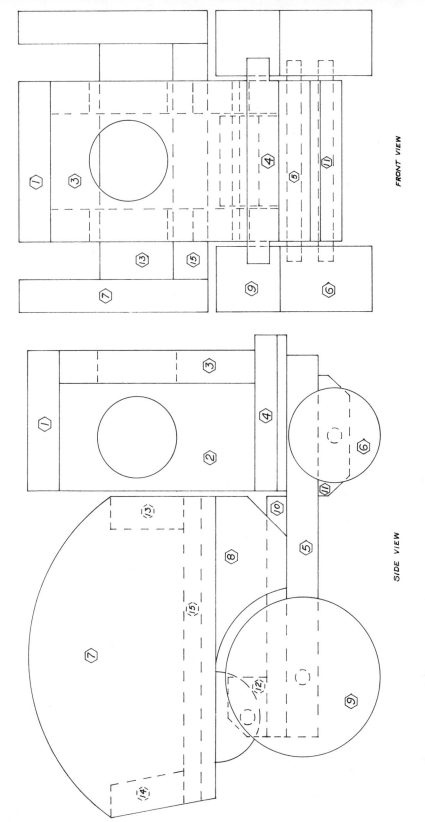

FRONT VIEW

SIDE VIEW

Figure 30–3 Side and front view of Dump Truck.

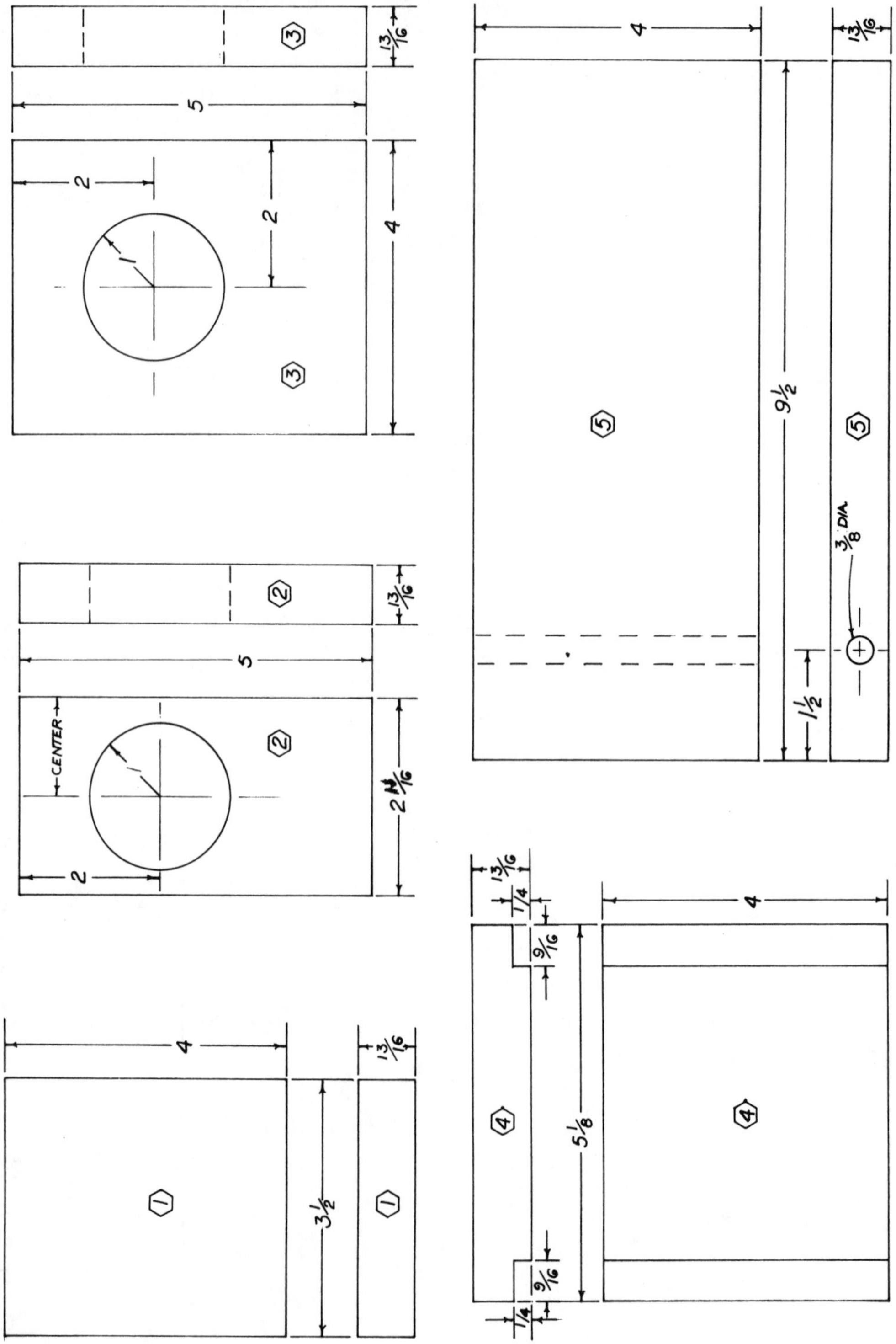

Figure 30–4 Dump Truck patterns.

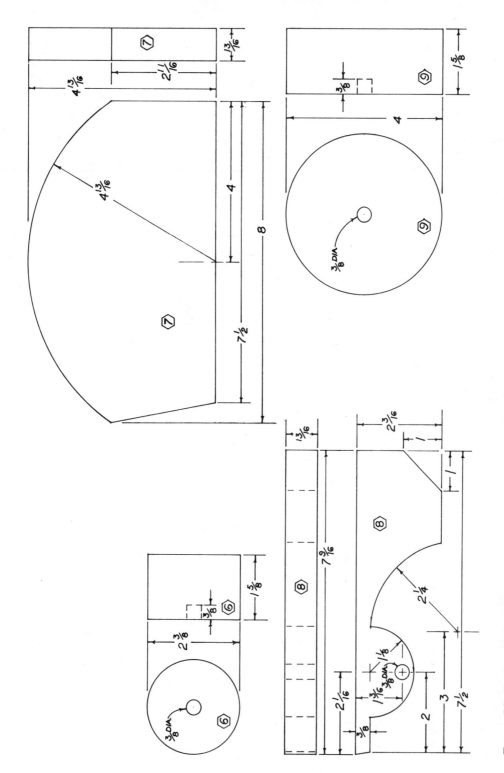

Figure 30–5 Dump Truck patterns.

215

Figure 30–6 Dump Truck patterns.

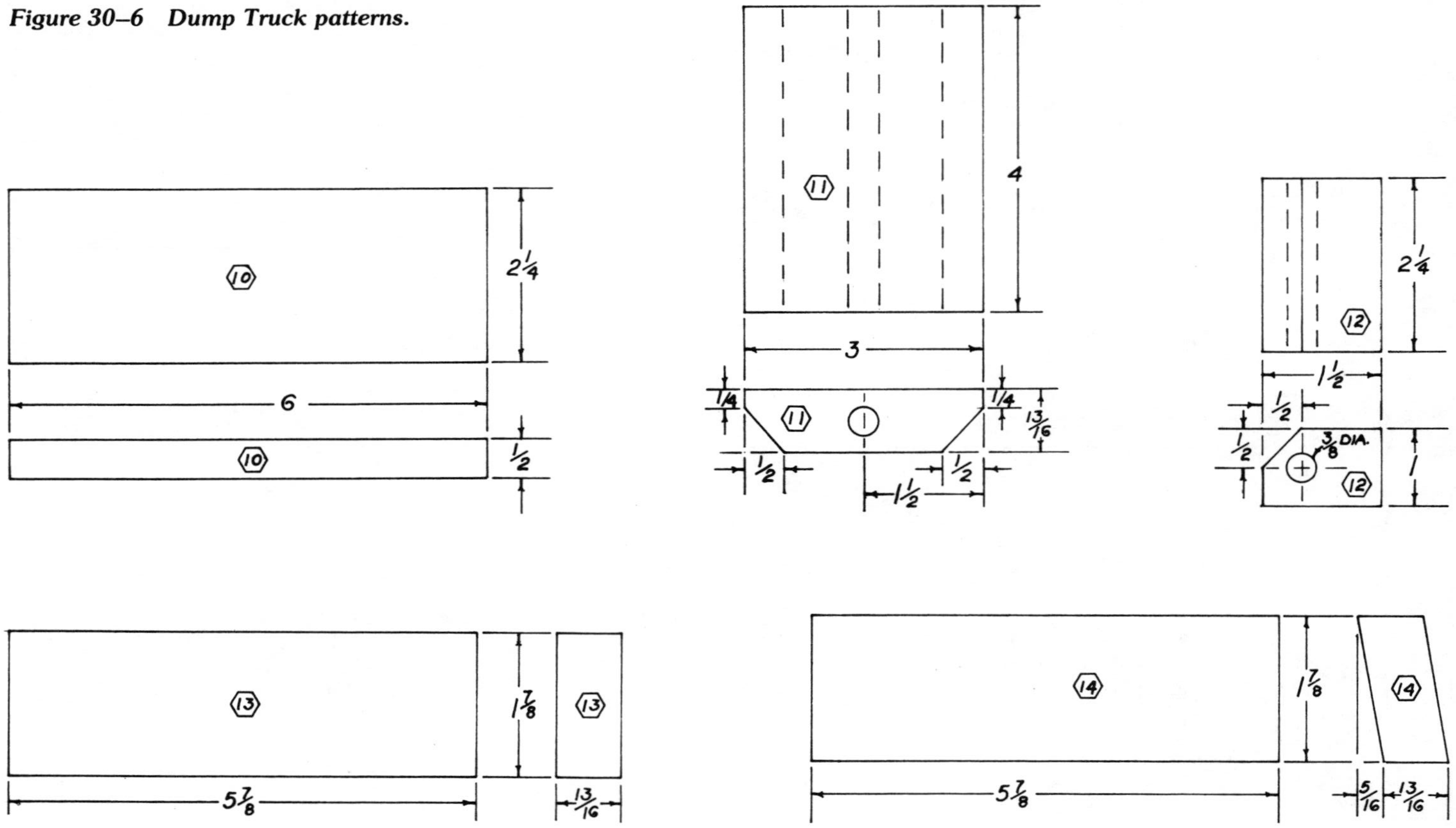

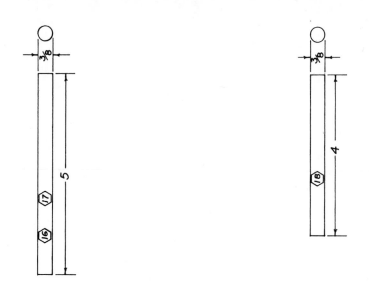

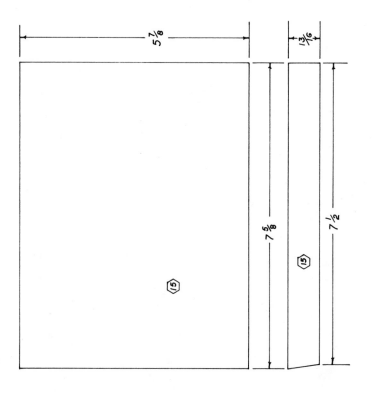

Figure 30–7 Dump Truck patterns.

Index

●